SIDE BY SIDE

English Grammar
Through
Guided Conversations
BOOK TWO

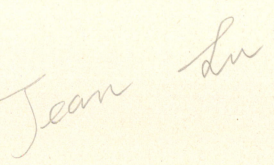

Jean Lu

SIDE BY SIDE

English Grammar Through Guided Conversations

BOOK TWO

Steven J. Molinsky

Bill Bliss

Illustrated by

Richard E. Hill

Prentice-Hall Inc., Englewood Cliffs, New Jersey 07632

Library of Congress Cataloging in Publication Data

MOLINSKY, STEVEN J
  Side by Side.

  Includes indexes.
    1. English language—Conversation and phrase books.
  2. English language—Text-books for foreigners.
  I. Bliss, Bill, joint author. II. Title.
  PE1131.M58   428.3′4   79-19946
  ISBN 0-13-809855-7 (v.2)

© 1981 by Prentice-Hall, Inc., Englewood Cliffs, N.J. 07632

Printed in the United States of America

10   9   8   7   6   5   4

Editorial/production supervisor: Penelope Linskey
Art/camera copy supervisor: Diane Heckler-Koromhas
Cover design by Suzanne Behnke
Manufacturing buyer: Harry P. Baisley

PRENTICE-HALL INTERNATIONAL, INC., *London*
PRENTICE-HALL OF AUSTRALIA PTY. LIMITED, *Sydney*
PRENTICE-HALL OF CANADA, LTD., *Toronto*
PRENTICE-HALL OF INDIA PRIVATE LIMITED, *New Delhi*
PRENTICE-HALL OF JAPAN, INC., *Tokyo*
PRENTICE-HALL OF SOUTHEAST ASIA PTE. LTD., *Singapore*
WHITEHALL BOOKS LIMITED, WELLINGTON, *New Zealand*

Contents

To the Teacher

Side by Side: Book Two is a conversational grammar book.

We do not seek to describe the language, nor prescribe its rules. Rather, we aim to help students learn to *use* the language grammatically, through practice with meaningful conversational exchanges.

This book is intended for adult and young-adult learners of English. It is designed to provide the intermediate-level student with the basic foundation of English grammar, through a carefully sequenced progression of conversational exercises and activities.

WHY A CONVERSATIONAL GRAMMAR BOOK?

Grammar is usually isolated and drilled through a variety of traditional structure exercises such as repetition, substitution, and transformation drills. Such exercises effectively highlight particular grammatical structures . . . but they are usually presented as a string of single sentences, not related to each other in any unifying, relevant context.

Traditional dialogues, on the other hand, may do a fine job of providing examples of real speech . . . but they don't usually offer sufficient practice with the structures being taught. Teachers and students are often frustrated by the lack of a clear grammatical focus in these meaningful contexts. Furthermore, it's hard to figure out what to *do* with a dialogue after you've read it, memorized it, or talked about it.

In this book we have attempted to combine the best features of traditional grammatical drills and contextually rich dialogues. The aim is to actively engage the students in meaningful conversational exchanges within carefully structured grammatical frameworks. The students are then encouraged to break away from the textbook and *use* these frameworks to create conversations *on their own*.

GRAMMATICAL PARADIGMS

Each lesson in the book covers one or more specific grammatical structures. A new structure appears first in the form of a grammatical paradigm, a simple schema of the structure.

These paradigms are to be a reference point for students as they proceed through the lesson's conversational activities. While these paradigms highlight the structures being taught, they are not intended to be goals in themselves.

We don't want our students simply to parrot back these rules: we want them to engage in conversations that show they can *use* them correctly.

GUIDED CONVERSATIONS

Guided Conversations are the dialogues and question-and-answer exchanges which are the primary learning devices in this book. Students are presented with a model conversation that highlights a specific aspect of the grammar. In the exercises that follow the model, students pair up and work "side by side," placing new content into the given conversational framework.

How to Introduce Guided Conversations

There are many ways to introduce these conversations. We don't want to dictate any particular method. Rather, we encourage you to develop strategies that are compatible with your own teaching style, the specific needs of your students, and the particular grammar and content of the lesson at hand.

Some teachers will want books closed at this stage, giving their students a chance to listen to the model before seeing it in print.

Other teachers will want students to have their books open for the model conversation or see it written on the blackboard. The teacher may read or act out the conversation while students follow along, or may read through the model with another student, or may have two students present the model to the class.

Whether books are open or closed, students should have ample opportunity to understand and practice the model before attempting the exercises that follow it.

How to Use Guided Conversations

In these conversational exercises, the students are asked to place new content into the grammatical and contextual framework of the model. The numbered exercises provide the student with new information which is "plugged into" the framework of the model conversation. Sometimes this framework actually appears as a "skeletal dialogue" in the text. Other times the student simply inserts the new information into the model that has just been practiced. (Teachers who have written the model conversation on the blackboard can create the skeletal dialogue by erasing the words that are replaced in the exercises.)

The teacher's key function is to pair up students for "side by side" conversational practice and then to serve as a resource to the class: for help with the structure, new vocabulary, and pronunciation.

"Side by side" practice can take many forms. Most teachers prefer to call on two students at a time to present a conversation to the class. Other teachers have their students pair up and practice the conversations together. Or small groups of students might work together, pairing up within these groups and presenting the conversations to each other.

This paired practice helps teachers address the varying levels of ability of their students. Some teachers like to pair stronger students with weaker ones. The slower student clearly gains through this pairing, while the more advanced student also strengthens his or her abilities by lending assistance to the speaking partner.

Other teachers will want to pair up or group students of *similar* levels of ability. In this arrangement, the teacher can devote greater attention to students who need it while giving more capable students the chance to learn from and assist each other.

While these exercises are intended for practice in conversation, teachers also find them useful as *writing* drills which reinforce oral practice and enable students to study more carefully the grammar highlighted in the conversations.

Once again, we encourage you to develop strategies that are most appropriate for your class.

The "Life Cycle" of a Guided Conversation

It might be helpful to define the different stages in the "life cycle" of a guided conversation.

I. *The Presentation Stage:*
The model conversation is introduced and is practiced by the class.

II. *The Rehearsal Stage:*
Immediately after practicing the model, students do the conversational exercises that follow it. For homework, they practice these conversations, and perhaps write out a few. Some lessons also ask students to create their own original conversations based on the model.

III. *The Performance Stage:*
The next day students do the conversational exercises in class, preferably with their textbooks and notebooks closed. Students shouldn't have to memorize these conversations. They will most likely remember them after sufficient practice in class and at home.

IV. The Incorporation Stage:
The class reviews the conversation or reviews pieces of the conversation in the days that follow. With repetition and time, the guided conversation "dissolves" and its components are incorporated into the student's active language.

ON YOUR OWN

An important component of each lesson is the On Your Own activity. These student-centered exercises reinforce the grammatical structures of the lesson while breaking away from the text and allowing students to contribute content of their own.

These activities take various forms: role-plays, extended guided conversations, questions about the student's real world, and topics for classroom discussion and debate. In these exercises the students are asked to bring new content to the classroom, based on their interests, their backgrounds, and the farthest reaches of their imaginations.

We recommend that the teacher read through these activities in class and assign them as homework for presentation the next day. In this way, students will automatically review the previous day's grammar while contributing new and inventive content of their own.

On Your Own activities are meant for simultaneous grammar reinforcement and vocabulary building. Students should be encouraged to use a dictionary when preparing these exercises. Thus, they will use not only the words they know, but the words they would *like* to know in order to bring their own interests, backgrounds, and imaginations into the classroom. As a result, students will be teaching each other new vocabulary and also sharing a bit of their lives with others in the class.

In conclusion, we have attempted to make the study of English grammar a lively and relevant experience for the student. While conveying to you the substance of our textbook, we hope that we have also conveyed the spirit: that learning the grammar can be conversational . . . student-centered . . . and fun.

Steven J. Molinsky
Bill Bliss

SIDE BY SIDE

English Grammar
Through
Guided Conversations
BOOK TWO

1

Review:

Simple Present Tense

Present Continuous Tense

Subject Pronouns

Object Pronouns

Possessive Adjectives

I	am	I'm		Am	I			I	am.
He		He's		Is	he			he	
She }	is	She's }			she		Yes,	she }	is.
It		It's			it	eating?		it	
	→	eating.		Are	we			we	
We		We're			you			you }	are.
You }	are	You're }			they			they	
They		They're							

Read and practice.

A. Are you busy?

B. Yes, I am. I'm studying.

A. What are you studying?

B. I'm studying English.

Complete these conversations using the model above.

1. Is Helen busy?
cooking spaghetti

2. Is Tom busy?
reading the newspaper

3. Are Bobby and Judy busy?
studying mathematics

4. Are you busy?
typing a letter

5. Are you and your brother busy?
cleaning the basement

6. Is Jane busy?
knitting a sweater

7. Are Mr. and Mrs. Watson busy?
baking cookies

8. Is Beethoven busy?
composing a new symphony

9. Is Whistler busy?
painting a portrait of his mother

| I
We
You
They } eat. |
| He
She
It } eats. |

| Do { I
we
you
they } |
| Does { he
she
it } eat? |

| Yes, { I
we
you
they } do. |
| { he
she
it } does. |

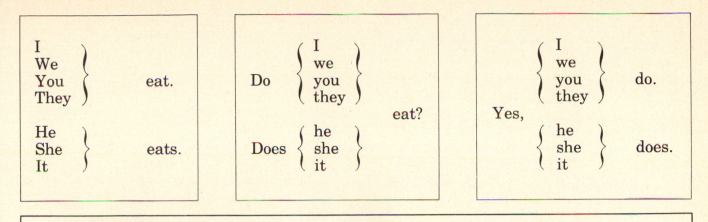

A. What are you doing?

B. I'm practicing the piano.

A. Do you practice the piano very often?

B. Yes, I do. I practice the piano whenever I can.

1. What's Edward doing?
bake bread

2. What's Janet doing?
swim

3. What are Mr. and Mrs. Green doing?
exercise

4. What are you doing?
read Shakespeare

5. What are you and your friend doing?
study English

6. What's Mary doing?
write to her grandparents

7. What's your neighbor doing?
play baseball with his son

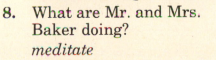

8. What are Mr. and Mrs. Baker doing?
meditate

9.

No, $\left\{\begin{array}{l} \text{I} \\ \text{we} \\ \text{you} \\ \text{they} \end{array}\right\}$ don't. (do not)

$\left\{\begin{array}{l} \text{he} \\ \text{she} \\ \text{it} \end{array}\right\}$ doesn't. (does not)

I'm not. (am not)

No, $\left\{\begin{array}{l} \text{he} \\ \text{she} \\ \text{it} \end{array}\right\}$ isn't. (is not)

$\left\{\begin{array}{l} \text{we} \\ \text{you} \\ \text{they} \end{array}\right\}$ aren't. (are not)

A. Do you like to ski?

B. No, I don't.
I'm not a very good skier.

1. Does Jim like to dance?
dancer

2. Does Rita like to sing?
singer

3. Do Mr. and Mrs. Brown like to skate?
skaters

4. Do you like to type?
typist

5. Do you and your friend like to play tennis?
tennis players

6. Does Shirley like to swim?
swimmer

7. Does David like to study?
student

8. Do you like to play sports?
athlete

I	my	me
he	his	him
she	her	her
it	its	it
we	our	us
you	your	you
they	their	them

A. Who are you calling?

B. **I'm** calling **my** brother in Chicago.

A. How often do you call **him**?

B. I call **him** every Sunday evening.*

A. What are George and Herman talking about?

B. **They're** talking about **their** grandchildren.

A. How often do they talk about **them**?

B. They talk about **them** all the time.*

*You can also say:
every day, week, weekend, month, year
every morning, afternoon, evening, night
every Sunday, Monday, . . . January, February, . . .

once a
twice a
three times a   } day, week, month, year
four times a
.
.
.
all the time

1. Who is Mrs. Lopez calling?
daughter in San Francisco

2. Who are you writing to?
uncle

3. Who is Walter visiting?
neighbors across the street

4. Who is Mrs. Morgan writing to?
son in the army

5. Who is Mr. Davis arguing with?
landlord

6. What are the students complaining about?
homework

抱怨，不满

7. What are you complaining about?
electric bill

8. Who is Mr. Crabapple shouting at?
employees

9. Who is Little Red Riding Hood visiting?
grandmother

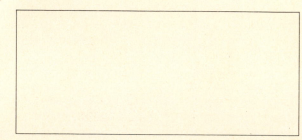

10.

1. Tell the class about yourself. Answer these questions and then ask other students:

Where are you from?
Where do you live now?
What do you do? (I'm a mechanic, a student . . .)
Where do you work/study?

2. Talk about the people in your family and ask other students about their families:

Are you married?   single?
Do you live with your parents?   Do you live alone?

3. Tell the class about your _____ (husband, wife, children, parents, brother(s), sister(s) . . .):

What are their names?
How old are they?
Where do they live?
What do they do?   Where?

4. Tell the class about your interests and ask other students about theirs:

Do you like to play sports?   cards?   chess? . . .?
How often do you go swimming?   play cards?   play chess? . . .?
What else do you like to do in your free time?

2

Review:
Simple Past Tense
(Regular and Irregular
Verbs)
Past Continuous Tense

What did	I he she it we you they	do?	I He She It We You They	worked.		

I He She It	was	
We You They	were	tired.

Read and practice.

A. Did Henry sleep well last night?

B. Yes, he did. He was VERY tired.

A. Why? What did he do yesterday?

B. He **cleaned his apartment** all day.

1. *you*
study English
studied

2. *Gloria*
work hard
worked

3. *David and Jeff*
wash windows
washed

4. *Miss Henderson*
teach
taught

5. *Mr. and Mrs. Warren*
look for an apartment
looked [t]

6. *Jack*
ride his bicycle
rode

7. *Irene*
write letters
wrote

8. *The President*
meet important people
met

9. _____

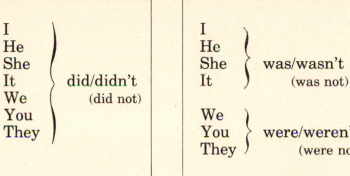

I / He / She / It / We / You / They	did/didn't (did not)

I / He / She / It	was/wasn't (was not)
We / You / They	were/weren't (were not)

A. Did Barney smoke a lot before his job interview?

B. Yes, he did. He was nervous.

A. Did Helen do well on her English exam?

B. No, she didn't. She wasn't prepared.

1. Did Marylou cry a lot when her dog ran away?

Yes, *she did. She was* upset.

2. Did Katherine sleep well last night?

No, she didn't. She wasn't tired.

3. Did you fall asleep during the lecture?

Yes, *I did. I was* bored.

4. Did Mr. and Mrs. Mason finish their dinner last night?

No, they didn't. They weren't hungry.

5. Did the football coach shout at his players after they lost the game?

Yes, *he did. He was* angry.

6. Did they have anything to drink after dinner last night?

No, they didn't. They weren't thirsty. 口渴

7. Did Tommy cover his eyes during the science fiction movie?

Yes, *he did. He was* scared.

8. Did George and his brother leave on the two o'clock train?

No, they didn't. They weren't on time.

afraid

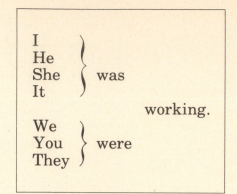

I He She It } was	
We You They } were	working.

A. How did John break his arm?

B. He broke it while he was **playing tennis**.

1. How did Sally break her leg?
ski down a mountain

2. How did Martin lose his wallet?
play baseball with his son

3. How did Peggy meet her husband?
read in the library one day

4. How did Mr. and Mrs. Thompson burn themselves?
bake cookies

5. How did Walter cut himself?
shave

6. How did Alan get a black eye?
argue with his neighbor

7. How did Martha cut herself?
prepare dinner

8. How did Rita rip her pants?
dance in a discotheque

9. How did Fred meet his wife?
wait for the bus one day

10. How did Presto the Magician hurt himself?
practice a new magic trick

ON YOUR OWN

Talk with other students in your class:
Do you remember how you met your (husband, wife, boyfriend, girlfriend, best friend)?

Where were you?
What were you doing?
What was he/she doing?

TELL ME ABOUT YOUR VACATION

1. Did you go to Paris?
No, we didn't.
Where did you go?
We went to Rome.

2. Did you get there by boat?
No, _____.
How _____?
_____ by plane.

3. Did your plane leave on time?
No, _____.
How late _____?
_____ two hours late.

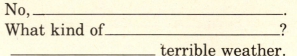

4. Did you have good weather during the flight?
No, _____.
What kind of _____?
_____ terrible weather.

5. Did you stay in a big hotel?
No, _____.
What kind of _____?
_____ a small hotel.

6. Did you eat in fancy restaurants?
No, _____.
Where _____?
_____ cheap restaurants.

7. Did you speak Italian?
No, _____.
What language _____?
_____ English.

8. Did you take many photographs?
No, _____.
How many _____?
_____ just a few photographs.

9. Did you buy any clothing?
No, _____.
What _____?
_____ souvenirs.

10. Did you swim in the Mediterranean?
No, _____.
Where _____?
_____ in the pool at our hotel.

11. Did you see the Colosseum?
No, _____.
What _____?
_____ the Vatican.

12. Did you travel around the city by taxi?
No, _____.
How _____?
_____ by bus.

13. Did you send postcards to your friends?

No, _____.

Who _____?

_____ our relatives.

14. Did you write to them about the monuments?

No, _____.

What _____?

_____ the weather.

15. Did you meet a lot of Italians?

No, _____.

Who _____?

_____ a lot of other tourists.

16. Did you come home by plane?

No, _____.

How _____?

_____ by boat.

ON YOUR OWN

Did you take a trip this year? Did you travel to another city?
Did you visit a friend or a relative out of town?
Talk with other students in your class about your last trip:

Where did you go?
How did you get there?
Where did you stay?
What did you do there?
How long were you there?
Did you have a good time?

If you have some photographs of your last trip, bring them to class and talk about them with the other students.

3

Review:
Future: Going to
Future: Will
Future Continuous Tense
Possessive Pronouns

I	am	
He		
She	is	going to read.
It		
We		
You	are	
They		

What am I going to do?

Where is he going to live?

Who are they going to call?

Expressions of Time

yesterday			last night
this	morning, afternoon, evening		tonight
tomorrow			tomorrow night

last		
this	week, month, year, Sunday, Monday, . . . spring, summer, . . .	
next	January, February, . . .	

Read and practice.

A. Are you going to plant carrots this year?

B. No, I'm not. I planted carrots LAST year.

A. What are you going to plant?

B. I'm going to plant tomatoes.

1. Is Ted going to wear his blue suit today?
his black suit

2. Is Barbara going to cook fish tonight?
chicken

3. Are you and your family going to go to Europe this summer?
Mexico

4. Is Charlie going to play popular music this evening?
jazz

5. Are you going to give your brother a watch for his birthday this year?
a tie

6. Are Mr. and Mrs. Peterson going to watch the football game on Channel 2 this Monday night?
the movie on Channel 4

7. Is Professor Hawkins going to teach European History this semester?
American History

8. Are you going to take ballet lessons this year?
tap dance lessons

9. Is Mrs. McCarthy going to buy grapes this week?
bananas

10. Are you going to call the landlord this time?
the plumber

I	will		I'll	
He	will		He'll	
She	will		She'll	
It	will	$\longrightarrow$	It'll	work.
We	will		We'll	
You	will		You'll	
They	will		They'll	

I		
He		
She		
It		won't work.
We		(will not)
You		
They		

A. Will Richard get out of the hospital soon?

B. Yes, he will. He'll get out in a few days.

A. Will Sherman get out of the hospital soon?

B. No, he won't. He won't get out for a few weeks.

1. Will the play begin soon?
Yes, _____ at 8:00.

2. Will the game begin soon?
No, _____ until 3:00.

3. Will Bob and Betty see each other again soon?
Yes, _____ this Saturday night.

4. Will John and Julia see each other again soon?
No, _____ until next year.

5. Will the soup be ready soon?
Yes, _____ in a few minutes.

6. Will the turkey be ready soon?
No, _____ for several hours.

7. Will Mom be back soon?
Yes, _____ in a little while.

8. Will Shirley be back soon?
No, _____ for a long time.

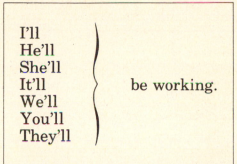

I'll
He'll
She'll
It'll
We'll
You'll
They'll
} be working.

A. Will you be home this evening?

B. Yes, I will.
I'll be **watching TV**.

A. Will Jane be home this evening?

B. No, she won't.
She'll be **working late at the office**.

1. *Tom*
read

2. *Mr. and Mrs. Harris*
paint their bathroom

3. *you*
swim

出租洗衣机店
LAUNDROMAT
[ˈlɔndrəmæt]

4. *Sheila*
do her laundry

5. *you and your family*
ice skate

6. *Sally*
clean her apartment

7. *Mr. and Mrs. Grant*
shop

8. *Donald*
fill out his
income tax form

9. *you*
visit a friend
in the hospital

A TELEPHONE CALL

Hi, _____. This is _____. Can you talk for a minute?

I'm sorry. I can't talk right now. I'm _____ing. Can you call back a little later?

Sure. How much longer will you be _____ing?

I'll probably be _____ing for another _____ minutes.

Fine. I'll call you in _____ minutes.

Speak to you soon.

Good-bye.

Complete this conversation and try it with another student in your class.

1. *study English*

2. *do my laundry*

3. *wash my kitchen floor*

4. *help my children with their homework*

5. *have dinner with my family*

6.

I	me	mine
he	him	his
she	her	hers
it	it	its
we	us	ours
you	you	yours
they	them	theirs

A. Could you possibly do me a favor? *+ 帮助力.*

B. Sure. I'll be happy to.

A. I've got a problem.
I have to fix my roof and I don't have a ladder.
Could I possibly borrow YOURS?

B. I'm sorry. I'm afraid I don't have one. *= I am sorry*

A. Do you know anybody who DOES?

B. Yes. You should call Charlie. I'm sure he'll be happy to lend you his.

A. Thank you. I'll call him right away. *= right now*

A. Could you possibly do me a favor?

B. Sure. I'll be happy to.

A. I've got a problem.
I have to _____ and I don't have a _____.
Could I possibly borrow YOURS?

B. I'm sorry. I'm afraid I don't have one.

A. Do you know anybody who DOES?

B. Yes. You should call _____. I'm sure _____'ll be happy to lend you
_____ (his, hers, theirs).

A. Thank you. I'll call _____ (him, her, them) right away.

1. *fix my TV set*
screwdriver 螺絲起子

2. *fix my front door*
hammer

3. *write a composition for my English class*
dictionary

4. *fix my flat tire*
jack

5. *go to a wedding*
tuxedo

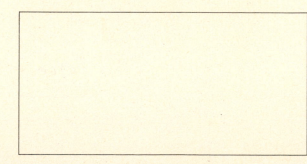

6.

Read and practice.

forward = be happy about something in the future.

1.

John is looking forward to this weekend. He isn't going to think about work. He's going to read a few magazines, fix his car, and <u>relax</u> at home with his family.

放鬆. 休息.

2.

Alice is looking forward to her birthday. Her sister is going to have a party for her and all her friends are going to be there.

3.

tent
backpack
sleeping bag
camera
flash light
hiking boots. radio. food. lamp

Mr. and Mrs. Williams are looking forward to their summer vacation. They're going to go camping in the mountains. They're going to hike 徒步 several miles every day, take a lot of pictures, and forget about all their problems at home.

4.

George is looking forward to his retirement. He's going to get up late every morning, visit friends every afternoon, and enjoy quiet evenings at home with his wife.

What are YOU looking forward to? A birthday? A holiday? A day off? Talk about it with other students in your class. 休假

What are you looking forward to?
When is it going to happen?
What are you going to do?

4

Present Perfect Tense

(past tense) I saw the movie yesterday. — you know the time

I have seen the movie this week. — you don't know the

(present perfect tense)   time.

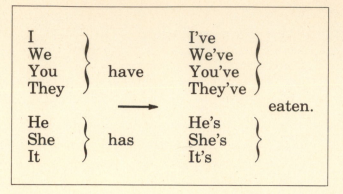

I			I've	
We	} have		We've	}
You			You've	
They			They've	
		→		eaten.
He			He's	
She	} has		She's	}
It			It's	

Read and practice.

A. Are Mr. and Mrs. Smith going to **see** a movie tonight?

B. No, they aren't. They've already **seen** a movie this week.

A. Really? When?

B. They **saw** a movie yesterday.

1. Are Mr. and Mrs. Smith going to eat at a restaurant tonight?
eat–ate–eaten

2. Is Frank going to get a haircut today?
get–got–gotten

3. Is Lucy going to write to her grandmother today?
write–wrote–written

4. Is Bob going to take his children to the zoo today?
take–took–taken

5. Are you going to give blood today?
give–gave–given

6. Are you and your friends going to see a play this evening?
see–saw–seen

7. Is Jennifer going to go to a concert tonight?
go–went–gone

8. Is Philip going to wear his red tie today?
wear–wore–worn

9. Is Mary going to do her laundry today?
do–did–done

10. Is Max going to swim at the health club today?
swim–swam–swum

11. Is Marion going to wash her car today?
wash–washed–washed

12. Is Jim going to bake cookies today?
bake–baked–baked

13. Are you going to buy bananas today?
buy–bought–bought

14. Is Tom going to spend a lot of money at the department store today?
spend–spent–spent

```
 I
 We  }  haven't
 You     (have not)
 They
                        eaten.*
 He
 She }  hasn't
 It     (has not)
```

A. Do you like to swim?

B. Yes, I do.   But I haven't swum in a long time.

A. Why not?

B. I just haven't had the time.

1. Does Kathy like to go to the zoo?

2. Does Robert like to <u>do</u> his English homework?

3. Do you like to <u>read</u> *The New York Times*?

4. Do you and your sister like to <u>bake</u> bread?

5. Do Bob and Sally like to <u>take</u> dance lessons?

6. Does Betsy like to <u>make</u> her own clothes?

7. Does William like to <u>write</u> poetry?

8. Do you like to <u>see</u> your old friends?

9.

yes, He does, written

*In the present perfect tense the word after **have** or **has** is a past participle.   Some past participles (**baked, bought, spent**) are the same as the past tense.   Other past participles (**eaten, taken, given**) are different from the past tense.   We will tell you when the past participles are different.   A list of these words is in the Appendix at the end of the book.

Have	I / we / you / they		eaten?
Has	he / she / it		

Yes,	I / we / you / they		have.
	he / she / it		has.

A. Have you **seen** the new Walt Disney movie yet?

B. Yes, I have. I **saw** it yesterday.

1. you *write your composition*
Have you written *wrote*

2. Nancy *ride her new bicycle**
Has Nancy ridden *rode*

3. Arthur *take his driver's test*
Has Arthur taken *took*

4. Sharon and Charles *do their homework*

5. you *read Chapter 3*
Have *read*

6. David *go to the bank*
Has David gone *went*

7. Mr. and Mrs. Chang *make plans for the weekend*
Have *made*

8. Stanley *wear his new suit*
Has *worn* *wore*

9. you *meet your new English teacher*
Have you met

*ride - rode - ridden

Have	I / we / you / they		
Has	he / she / it		eaten?

No,	I / we / you / they		haven't.
	he / she / it		hasn't.

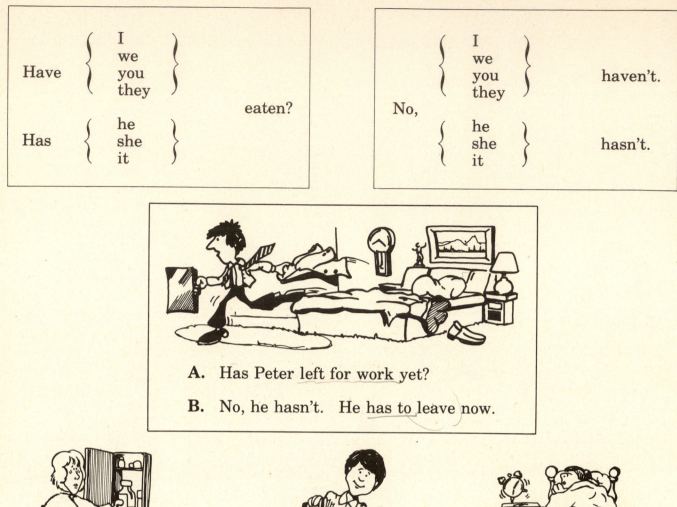

A. Has Peter left for work yet?

B. No, he hasn't. He has to leave now.

1. *Mildred*
take her medicine

2. *you*
finish your homework

3. *Bill*
get up

4. *John and Julia*
say good-bye

5. *you*
feed the dog

6. *Barbara*
call her boss

7. *Timmy*
go to bed

8. *you*
*speak to your landlord**

9. *Harry*
pay his electric bill

*speak - spoke - spoken

Read and practice.

A. What are you going to do tonight?

B. I'm not sure. I really want to see a good movie. I haven't seen a good movie in a long time.

A. What movie are you going to see?

B. I don't know. Have you seen any good movies recently?

A. Yes, I have. I saw a VERY good movie just last week.

B. Really? What movie did you see?

A. I saw *Gone with the Wind*.

B. And you liked it?

A. I LOVED it! I think it's one of the BEST movies I've ever seen.

A. What are you going to do tonight?

B. I'm not sure. I really want to _____ a good _____.
I haven't _____ a good _____ in a long time.

A. What _____ are you going to _____?

B. I don't know. Have you _____ any good _____s recently?

A. Yes, I have. I _____ a VERY good _____ just last week.

B. Really? What _____ did you _____?

A. I _____ "_____."

B. And you liked it?

A. I LOVED it! I think it's one of the BEST _____s I've ever _____.

1. *see – play*

2. *read – book*

3. *eat at – restaurant*

4. *go to – discotheque**

*Or: nightclub, cafe.

5

Present Perfect vs.
Present Tense
Present Perfect vs.
Past Tense
For, Since

for	since
three hours	three o'clock
two days	yesterday afternoon
a week	last week
a long time	1960
•	•
•	•
•	•

Read and practice.

A. How long have you known*each other?

B. We've known each other **for two years**.

*know - knew - known

A. How long have you been sick?

B. I've been sick **since last Thursday**.

1. How long have Mr. and Mrs. Jones known each other?

   for **three years**

2. How long have Mr. and Mrs. Peterson been married?

   since **1945**

3. How long has Tommy liked girls?

since last year

4. How long has Diane had problems with her back?

for two years

5. How long have you had a headache?

since ten o'clock this morning

6. How long has Mrs. Brown been a teacher?

for thirteen years

7. How long have there been satellites in space?

since 1957

8. How long have you owned this car?

for five and a half years

9. How long has John owned his own house?

since 1971

10. How long have you been interested in astronomy?

for many years

11. How long has Lucy been interested in computer technology?

for a long time

12. How long have you been here?

since 1963

jail — short

prison — long

A. Do you know Mrs. Potter?

B. Yes, I do. I've known her for a long time.

A. How long have you known her?

B. I've known her **since I was a little boy**.

A. Are you two engaged?

B. Yes, we are. We've been engaged for a long time.

A. How long have you been engaged?

B. We've been engaged **since we finished high school**.

1. Does your brother play the piano?
since he was eight years old

2. Is your friend Victor a professional musician?
since he finished college

3. Do you have a fever? *yes, I do, I have had a fever*
since I got up yesterday morning

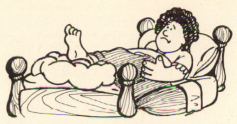

4. Does Mary's leg hurt?
since she fell down on the sidewalk last week

5. Are you interested in modern art?
since I read about Picasso 畫家畢卡索

6. Is Jeffrey interested in French history?
since he visited Paris

7. Do you like jazz?
since I was a teenager

8. Do you know how to ski?
since we were very young

9. Does Johnny know how to count to ten?
since he was two years old

10. Is your brother married?
since he got out of the army

11. Do you want to be an actress?
since I saw "Gone with the Wind"

12. Do your children know about "the birds and the bees"?*
since they were nine years old

*the facts of life.

A. Has Ralph always been a carpenter?

B. No, he hasn't.
He's been a carpenter for the last ten years.
Before that, **he was** a painter.

A. Have you always taught history?

B. No, I haven't.
I've taught history since 1970.
Before that, **I taught** geography.

1. Has Fred always been thin?
for *the last three years*

2. Has Roberta always had short hair?
since *she finished college*

3. Have you always liked classical music?
for *the past few years*

4. Have your parents always been Democrats?
since *Watergate**

*an American political scandal in 1973–74.

40

5. Has Steven always spoken with a Boston accent?

since *he moved to Boston*

6. Have you always had a dog?

for *the past five or six years*

7. Has Andy always wanted to be an astronaut?

since *last September*

8. Has Louis always been the store manager?

for *the last six months*

9. Has Janet always known all the people in her apartment building?

since *the fire last year*

10. Has Larry always owned a sports car?

since *he won the lottery*

Answer these questions and then ask other students in your class.

1. What is your present address?
How long have you lived there?

2. What was your last address?
How long did you live there?

3. Who is the President/Prime Minister of your country?
How long has he/she been the President/Prime Minister?

4. Who was the last President/Prime Minister of your country?
How long was he/she the President/Prime Minister?

5. Who is your English teacher now?
How long has he/she been your English teacher?

6. Who was your last English teacher?
How long was he/she your English teacher?

Read and practice.

IT'S BEEN A LONG TIME

A. George!

B. Tony! I can't believe it's you! I haven't seen you in years.

A. That's right, George. It's been a long time. How have you been?

B. Fine. And how about YOU?

A. Everything's fine with me, too.

B. Tell me, Tony. Do you still live on Main Street?

A. No. I haven't lived on Main Street for several years.

B. Where do you live NOW?

A. I live on River Road. And how about YOU? Do you still live on Central Avenue?

B. No. I haven't lived on Central Avenue since 1975.

A. Where do you live NOW?

B. I live on Park Boulevard.

A. Tell me, George. Are you still a barber?

B. No. I haven't been a barber for several years.

A. Really? What do you do NOW?

B. I'm a taxi driver. And how about YOU? Are you still a painter?

A. No. I haven't been a painter for a long time.

B. Really? What do you do NOW?

A. I'm a carpenter.

B. Tell me, Tony. Do you still play the violin?

A. No. I haven't played the violin for many years. And how about YOU? Do you still go fishing on Saturday mornings?

B. No. I haven't gone fishing on Saturday mornings since I got married.

A. Well, George. I'm afraid I have to go now. We should get together soon.

B. Good idea, Tony. It's been a long time.

Pretend that it's ten or fifteen years from now. You're walking along the street and suddenly you meet a student who was in your English class. Try this conversation. Remember, you haven't seen this person for ten or fifteen years.

A. _____!

B. _____! I can't believe it's you! I haven't seen you in years.

A. That's right, _____. It's been a long time. How have you been?

B. Fine. And how about YOU?

A. Everything's fine with me, too.

B. Tell me, _____. Do you still live on _____?

A. No. I haven't lived on _____ (for/since) _____.

B. Where do you live NOW?

A. I live on _____. And how about YOU? Do you still live on _____?

B. No. I haven't lived on _____ (for/since) _____.

A. Where do you live NOW?

B. I live on _____.

A. Tell me, _____. Are you still a _____?

B. No. I haven't been a _____ (for/since) _____.

A. Really? What do you do NOW?

B. I'm a _____. And how about YOU? Are you still a _____?

A. No. I haven't been a _____ (for/since) _____.

B. Really? What do you do NOW?

A. I'm a _____.

B. Tell me, _____. Do you still _____?

A. No. I haven't _____ (for/since) _____.
And how about YOU? Do you still _____?

B. No. I haven't _____ (for/since) _____.

A. Well, _____. I'm afraid I have to go now. We should get together soon.

B. Good idea, _____. It's been a long time.

6

Present Perfect
Continuous Tense

I			I've	
We			We've	
You	}	have	You've	
They			They've	
		⟶		been working.
He			He's	
She	}	has	She's	
It			It's	

Read and practice.

A. How long have you been waiting?

B. I've been waiting for two hours.

A. How long has Henry been working at the post office?

B. He's been working at the post office since 1957.

1. How long have you been feeling bad?

since *yesterday morning*

2. How long has Nancy been playing the piano?

for *several years*

3. How long has the phone been ringing?

for *five minutes*

4. How long have Mr. and Mrs. Brown been living on Appleton Street?

since *1948*

5. How long has Maria been studying English?

for *ten months*

6. How long has Frank been going out with Sally?

for *three and a half years*

7. How long have you been having problems with your back?

since *high school*

8. How long have we been driving?

for *seven hours*

9. How long has it been snowing?

since *late last night*

10. How long has your baby son been crying?

since *early this morning*

11. How long have they been building the new bridge?

for *two years*

swim trunks suit

12. How long has Arnold been lying in the sun?

since *twelve noon*

Have $\begin{Bmatrix} I \\ we \\ you \\ they \end{Bmatrix}$

Has $\begin{Bmatrix} he \\ she \\ it \end{Bmatrix}$ been working?

A. What are your neighbors doing?

B. They're arguing.

A. Have they been arguing for a long time?

B. Yes, they have. They've been arguing all day.*

*You can also say: all morning, all afternoon, all evening, all night.

1. *you*
studying

2. *Robert*
ironing

3. *Laura*
waiting for the bus

4. *you and your friends*
standing in line for
concert tickets

5. *Ricky*
talking to his girlfriend

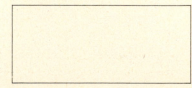

6. *Jane*
looking for her keys

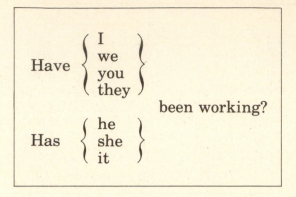

7. *Mr. and Mrs. Wilson*
washing their windows

8. *your car* *What is your* **9.**
making strange noises *car doing?*

A. You look tired.* What have you been doing?

B. I've been writing letters since ten o'clock this morning.

A. Really? How many letters have you written?

B. Believe it or not, I've already written fifteen letters.

A. Fifteen letters?! NO WONDER you're tired!

A. Mary looks tired.* What has she been doing?

B. She's been baking cakes since nine o'clock this morning.

A. Really? How many cakes has she baked?

B. Believe it or not, she's already baked seven cakes.

A. Seven cakes?! NO WONDER she's tired!

*You can also say: exhausted.

1. *you*
wash windows

2. *Dr. Anderson*
see patients

3. Miss Shultz
give piano lessons

4. Mr. and Mrs. Johnson
buy Christmas presents

5. you
pick apples

6. Mr. Williams
plant flowers

7. your grandmother
mend socks

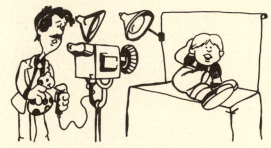

8. Bob
take photographs

9. you and your friends
review our English lessons

10. Jennifer
write thank-you notes

11. John
go to job interviews

12. you
fill out income tax forms

A. I'm nervous.

B. Why?*

A. I'm going to **fly in an airplane** tomorrow, and I've never **flown in an airplane** before.

B. Don't worry! I've been **flying in airplanes** for years. And believe me, there's nothing to be nervous about!

1. *buy a used car*

2. *have a party*

3. *drive† downtown*

4. *go to a job interview*

5. *give blood*

6. *take a karate lesson*

*You can also say: How come?

†**drive–drove–driven**

[kə`rɑti] 空手道

51

7. *speak at a meeting*

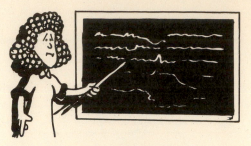

8. *teach an English class*

9. *run*in a marathon*

10. *sing† in front of an audience*

11. *ask for a raise*

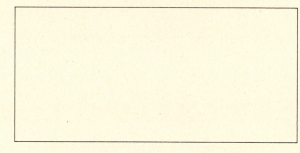

12.

Answer these questions and ask other students in your class.

1. Have you ever flown in an airplane?
(Where did you go?)

2. Have you ever been in the hospital?
(Why were you there?)

3. Have you ever met a famous person?
(Who did you meet?)

4. Have you ever been very embarrassed?
(What happened?) [ɪmˈbærəs] 使困窘，使侷促不安

5. Have you ever been in an accident?
(What happened?)

6. _____?

7. _____?

*run–ran–run
†sing–sang–sung 起入賽[marathon]

Complete this conversation and act it out with another student in your class.

AT THE DOCTOR'S OFFICE

A. How are you feeling, (Mr./Mrs./Miss/Ms.) _____?

B. Well, Doctor. I've been having problems with my _____.

A. I'm sorry to hear that. How long have you been having problems with your _____?

B. (For/Since)_____.

A. Have you ever had problems with your _____ before?

B. No. Never. This is the first time.

A. Tell me, (Mr./Mrs./Miss/Ms.) _____. Have you been sleeping O.K.?

B. No, Doctor. I haven't had a good night's sleep since my _____ began to bother me.

A. And how about your appetite? Have you been eating well lately?

B. { Yes, I have. }
{ No, I haven't. }

A. What have you been eating?

B. I've been eating _____.

(after the examination)

A. Well, (Mr./Mrs./Miss/Ms.) _____. I think you should _____.*

B. Do you think that will help?

A. Yes, indeed. A lot of people have been coming to me lately with _____ problems, and I've been advising all of them to _____.

B. Thank you, Doctor. You've been a great help.

A. It's been a pleasure, (Mr./Mrs./Miss/Ms.) _____. I'm sure you'll be feeling better soon.

*take aspirin three times a day; exercise more; drink a lot of water;
rest in bed for a few days; see a specialist;...

7

Gerunds

Infinitives

Review: Present Perfect and Present Perfect Continuous Tenses

to read	reading
to dance	dancing
to swim	swimming

Read and practice.

A. Do you **like to watch TV**?

B. Yes. I **enjoy watching TV** very much.
Watching TV is my favorite way to relax.

1. *you*
listen to music

2. *Tom*
swim

3. *Lucy*
read

4. *you and your friends*
dance

5. *Mr. and Mrs. Green*
play tennis

6. *you*
ice skate

7. *Shirley*
sew [so]

8. *Alan*
play chess

9. *your parents*
go to the movies

{ like to work } { like working }	{ can't stand to work }* { can't stand working }	{ — } { avoid working }

A. Does Ronald like { **to travel** / **traveling** } by plane?

B. No. He **can't stand** { **to travel** / **traveling** } by plane.

He **avoids traveling** by plane whenever he can.

1. *Sally*
do her homework

2. *Mr. and Mrs. Simon*
drive downtown

3. *you*
talk on the telephone

4. *Jim*
work late at the office

5. *you and your friends*
talk about politics

6. *Julie*
eat spinach

7. *you*
practice the piano

8. *Michael*
visit his mother-in-law

9. *Mr. and Mrs. Kendall*
play cards with their
neighbors

Ask another student: What do you enjoy doing?
What do you avoid doing whenever you can?

*You can also say:
{ **hate to work** }
{ **hate working** }

A. How did you **learn to swim** so well?

B. I **started** { **to swim** / **swimming** } when I was young, and I've been **swimming** ever since.

A. I envy you. I've never **swum** before.

B. I'll be glad to teach you how.

A. Thank you.* But isn't **swimming** very difficult?

B. Not at all. After you **practice swimming** a few times, you'll probably **swim** as well as I do.

*You can also say: I appreciate that. That's very kind of you. That's very nice of you.

jealous
忌妒 羡慕

A. How did you learn to _____ so well?

B. I started { to _____ / _____ing } when I was young, and I've been _____ing ever since.

A. I envy you. I've never _____ before.

B. I'll be glad to teach you how.

A. Thank you.* But isn't _____ing very difficult?

B. Not at all. After you practice _____ing a few times, you'll probably _____ as well as I do.

1. *draw†*

2. *ski*

3. *figure skate*

4. *bake bread*

5. *tap dance*

6. *play chess*

7. *box*

8.

*You can also say: I appreciate that. That's very kind of you. That's very nice of you.
†**draw–drew–drawn**

A. Guess what I've decided to do!

B. I can't guess. What?

A. I've **decided to get married**.

B. You HAVE? That's GREAT!
How long have you been **thinking about getting married**?

A. For a long time, actually.
I **considered getting married** YEARS ago, but I never did.

B. Why have you **decided to get married** NOW?

A. I've decided that if I don't **get married** now, I never will.
Do you think I'm making the right decision?

B. Yes, I do. I think **getting married** is a WONDERFUL idea!

A. I'm glad you think so.

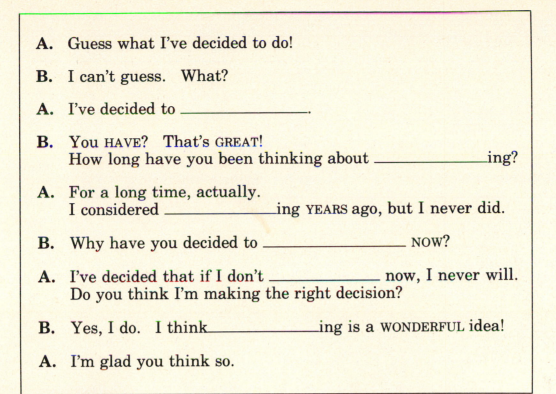

A. Guess what I've decided to do!

B. I can't guess. What?

A. I've decided to _____.

B. You HAVE? That's GREAT!
How long have you been thinking about _____ing?

A. For a long time, actually.
I considered _____ing YEARS ago, but I never did.

B. Why have you decided to _____ NOW?

A. I've decided that if I don't _____ now, I never will.
Do you think I'm making the right decision?

B. Yes, I do. I think _____ing is a WONDERFUL idea!

A. I'm glad you think so.

1. *move to Chicago*

2. *buy a new car*

3. *get a dog*

4. *go on a diet*

5. *grow a beard**

6. *go back to college*

7. *start my own business*

8.

*grow–grew–grown

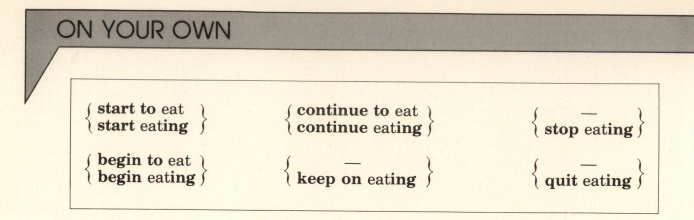

{ start **to** eat / start eat**ing** }	{ continue **to** eat / continue eat**ing** }	{ — / stop eat**ing** }
{ begin **to** eat / begin eat**ing** }	{ — / keep on eat**ing** }	{ — / quit eat**ing** }

Complete this conversation and try it with another student in your class.

A. I have some good news!

B. What is it?

A. I've decided to stop* _____ing.

B. That's GREAT! Do you really think you'll be able to do it?

A. I think so. But it won't be easy.
I've been _____ing for a long time.

B. Have you ever tried to stop _____ing before?

A. Yes. Many times. But every time I've stopped _____ing,
I've started† { to _____ / _____ing } again after a few days.

B. I hope you'll be successful this time.

A. I hope so, too.
After all, I can't keep on‡ _____ing for the rest of my life!

I can come — present
I could come — past
I will be able to come — future

1. *smoke*
2. *gamble*
3. *eat junk food*
4.

*You can also say: quit.
†You can also say: **begin–began–begun.**
‡You can also say: continue.

8

Past Perfect Tense

Past Perfect Continuous Tense

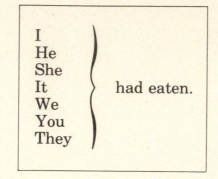

I He She It We You They	had eaten.

Read and practice.

the weekend before

A. Did Mr. and Mrs. Jones **drive** to the beach last weekend?

B. No. They didn't want to.
They **had** just **driven** to the beach the weekend before.

the night before

had just seen

1. Did Mr. and Mrs. Henderson see a movie last Saturday night?

They

the evening before

had just eaten

2. Did George eat at a restaurant yesterday evening?

the week before

had just taken

3. Did Rosa take a day off last week?

the weekend before

had just gone

4. Did you go skiing last weekend?

64

(the week before)

the Sunday before

had just had

5. Did you and your friends have a picnic last Sunday? *We*

the night before

6. Did Shirley have pizza for dinner last night? *She had just had*

the year before

had taken

7. Did Gregory take a geography course last year? *He*

the weekend before

had given

8. Did Helen give a party last weekend? *She*

the evening before

ted

9. Did Mr. and Mrs. Stevens discuss politics at the dinner table yesterday evening? *They*

the day before

had gone

10. Did you go window-shopping last Saturday? *I*

the week before

11. Did Mabel bake one of her delicious apple pies last week? *She*

worn the day before 图图花纹

12. Did Philip wear his polka dot shirt to work last Tuesday?

No, He didn't want to. He had just worn his polka dot shirt

the weekend before

13. Did Stanley do magic tricks for his friends last weekend? 魔术特技

14.

A. Did you get to the **plane** on time?

B. No, I didn't.
By the time I got to the **plane**, it had already **taken off**.

1. concert
   begin

2. post office
   close

3. train
   leave

4. lecture
   end

5. movie
   start

6. meeting
   finish

7. bank
   close

8. boat
   sail away

9. parade
   go by

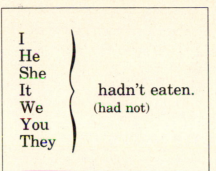

I He She It We You They	**hadn't eaten.** (had not)

A. Did George enjoy **seeing his old friends** last night?

B. Yes, he did. He hadn't **seen his old friends** in a long time.

1. Did you enjoy swimming in the ocean last weekend?

2. Did Janice enjoy singing with the choir last Sunday?

3. Did Mr. and Mrs. Gleason enjoy taking a walk along the beach yesterday?

4. Did you and your friends enjoy going out for dinner last night?

5. Did Susan enjoy visiting her grandparents last Sunday afternoon?

6. Did Andrew and Eric enjoy having chocolate cake for dessert last night?

7. Did Professor Nelson enjoy seeing his former students last week?

8. Did Walter enjoy playing "hide and seek" with his children last night?

9. Did Mrs. Thompson enjoy reading her old love letters last weekend?

A. Have you heard about Harry?

B. No, I haven't. What happened?

A. He broke his leg last week.

B. That's terrible! How did he do that?

A. He was playing soccer . . . and he had never played soccer before.

B. Poor Harry! I hope he feels better soon.

A. Have you heard about _____?

B. No, I haven't. What happened?

A. (He/She) _____ last week.

B. That's terrible! How did (he/she) do that?

A. (He/She) was _____ing . . . and (he/she) had never _____ before.

B. Poor _____! I hope (he/she) feels better soon.

Tom

1. *twist his ankle*
    fly a kite*

Doris

2. *sprain her wrist*
    play tennis

*fly–flew–flown

Vincent

3. *burn himself*
bake chocolate chip cookies

Peggy

4. *get hurt in an accident*
ride on a motorcycle

Edward

5. *get a black eye*
box

Stella

6. *injure her knee*
wrestle

Rover

7. *break his front teeth*
chew on a steak bone

Irene

8. *lose her voice*
sing opera

Brian

9. *sprain his back*
do the tango

10.

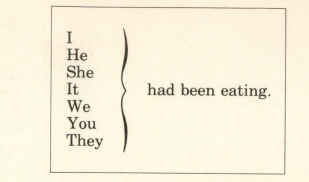

I	
He	
She	
It	} had been eating.
We	
You	
They	

A. I heard that Arnold failed his driver's test last week.
Is it true?

B. Yes, it is . . . and it's really a shame.
He had been practicing for a long time.

A. I heard that _____ last week.
Is it true?

B. Yes, it is . . . and it's really a shame.
(He/She/They) had been _____ing for a long time.

I heard that . . .

1. Lucy lost her job at the bank
work there

2. Boris lost the chess match
practice

3. Ted and Carol broke up
go together

4. Robert did poorly on his English examination
study for it

5. Sally had to cancel her trip to Canada
plan it

6. Dick and Janet cancelled their wedding
plan to get married

7. Mrs. Gold had another heart attack
feel better

8. Mr. and Mrs. Hardy moved
live in this neighborhood

9. Lisa got sick and couldn't see the parade
hope to see it

10. Roger caught a cold and couldn't go camping
look forward to it

Read and practice.

1.

Patty had planned to have a party last weekend. She had been getting ready for the party for a long time. She had invited all of her friends. She had cooked lots of food. And she had cleaned her apartment from top to bottom. But at the last minute, she got sick and had to cancel her party. Poor Patty! She was really disappointed.

2.

Michael had planned to ask his boss for a raise last week. He had been preparing to ask his boss for a raise for a long time. He had come to work early for several weeks. He had worked late at the office every night. And he had even bought a new suit to wear to the appointment with his boss. Unfortunately, before Michael could even ask for a raise, his boss fired him.

3.

John and Julia had planned to get married last month. They had been planning their wedding for several months, and all of their friends and relatives had been looking forward to the ceremony. Julia had bought a beautiful wedding gown. John had rented a fancy tuxedo. And they had sent invitations to 150 people. But at the last minute, John "got cold feet"* and they had to cancel the wedding.

Talk with other students in your class about plans YOU had that "fell through":

What had you planned to do?
How long had you been planning to do it?
What had you done beforehand?
What went wrong? (What happened?)
Were you upset? disappointed?

*You can also say: got scared.

9

Two-Word Verbs:
Separable
Inseparable

SEPARABLE TWO-WORD VERBS

bring back the book	**bring** it **back**
call up Sally	**call** her **up**
put on your boots	**put** them **on**

Read and practice.

A. When is the repairman going to **bring back** your television?

B. He's going to **bring** it **back** sometime next week.

1. When are you going to **call up** your cousin in Chicago?

2. When is John going to **fill out** his income tax form?

3. When is Greta going to **pick up** her clothes at the cleaner's?

4. When is Maria going to **pick out** her wedding gown?

5. When are you going to **put away** your winter clothes?

6. When is Peter going to **bring back** his library books?

7. When is your landlord going to **turn on** the heat?

8. When is Margaret going to **throw out** her old magazines?

9. When are you going to **hang up** your new portrait?

$$\begin{cases} \textbf{put on } \text{your boots} \\ \textbf{put } \text{your boots } \textbf{on} \end{cases} \textbf{put } \text{them } \textbf{on}$$

A. Did you remember to $\begin{cases} \textbf{turn off } \text{the oven} \\ \textbf{turn } \text{the oven } \textbf{off} \end{cases}$?

B. Oh, no! I completely forgot!
I'll **turn** it **off** right away.

1. *bring back
your library books*

2. *put away
your toys*

3. *call up
your Aunt Gertrude*

4. *fill out
your income tax form*

5. *hand in
your English homework*

6. *take out
the garbage*

7. *take off
your boots*

8. *put on
your raincoat*

9. *turn on
the "no smoking" sign*

A. Do you think I should keep these old love letters?

B. No, I don't.*
I think you should **throw** them **away**.

*You can also say: No, I don't think so. Not really. That probably isn't a very good idea.

1. *keep my ex-boyfriend's ring*
give back

2. *leave the air-conditioner on*
turn off

3. *hand my homework in*
do over

4. *erase all my mistakes*
cross out

5. *throw out this old milk*
use up

6. *try to remember Sally's telephone number*
write down

7. *make my decision right away*
think over

8. *accept my new job offer*
turn down

9. *ask the teacher the definition of this new word*
look up

Read and practice.

Hi, Paul. This it Tom.
Would you like to get together today?

I'm afraid I can't.
I have to **fill out** my income tax form.

Are you free after you **fill** it **out**?

I'm afraid not.
I also have to **bring** my library books **back**.

Would you like to get together after you **bring** them **back**?

I'd really like to, but I can't.
I ALSO have to **pick** my sister **up** at the airport.

You're really busy today!
What do you have to do after you **pick** her **up**?

Nothing. But by then I'll probably be EXHAUSTED!
Let's get together tomorrow instead.

Fine. I'll call you in the morning.

Speak to you then.

A. Hi, _____. This is _____.
Would you like to get together today?

B. I'm afraid I can't.
I have to _____.

A. Are you free after you _____?

B. I'm afraid not.
I also have to _____.

A. Would you like to get together after you _____?

B. I'd really like to, but I can't.
I ALSO have to _____.

A. You're really busy today!
What do you have to do after you _____?

B. Nothing. But by then I'll probably be EXHAUSTED!
Let's get together tomorrow instead.

A. Fine. I'll call you in the morning.

B. Speak to you then.

1.

2.

☑ **clean up** my room

☑ **put away** my clothes

☑ **do over** my Algebra homework

3.

☑ **take down** my Christmas decorations

☑ **hang up** my New Year's party decorations

☑ **drop off** my suit at the cleaner's

4.

☑ **figure out** my hospital bill

☑ **fill out** my insurance form

☑ **call up** the doctor

Using any of the two-word verbs in this chapter, try this conversation with another student in your class.

5.

☑ _____

☑ _____

☑ _____

INSEPARABLE TWO-WORD VERBS

call on John   **call on** him
~~call John on~~   ~~call him on~~

A. Have you **heard from** your Uncle George recently?

B. Yes, I have. As a matter of fact, I **heard from** him just last week.*

*You can also say: the other day,   a few days ago,   a few minutes ago . . .

1. Have you **heard from** your cousin Betty recently?

2. Have you **looked through** your old English book recently?

3. Have you **run into** Mr. Smith recently?

4. Have you **gotten over** the flu yet?

5. Has your English teacher **called on** you recently?

6. Have you been **picking on** your little brother lately?

TALK ABOUT SOME OF THE PEOPLE IN YOUR LIFE

Answer these questions and then ask other students in your class.

1. Do you have a good friend in another city? Who is he/she? How often do you **hear from** him/her? How long have you known each other?

2. Who do you **get along with** very well? Why?

3. Who do you **take after**? How?

4. Who do you **look up to**? Why?

Complete this conversation and act it out with another student in your class.

IN THE DEPARTMENT STORE

A. May I help you?

B. Yes, please. I'm **looking for** a _____.

A. What size do you wear?

B. I'm not sure. I think I take a size _____.

A. Here's a nice size _____. How do you like (it/them)?

B. I think (it's/they're) a little too _____.*
Do you have any _____s that are a little _____er?*

A. Yes. We have a wide selection.
Why don't you **look through** all of our _____s on your own and
pick out the (one/ones) you like.

B. Can I **try** (it/them) **on**?

A. Of course. You can **try** (it/them) **on** $\left\{ \begin{array}{l} \text{right here.} \\ \text{in the dressing room} \\ \text{over there.} \end{array} \right\}$

*
fancy–plain (dull)
dark–light

(5 minutes later)

A. Well, how $\left(\begin{array}{l}\text{does it}\\\text{do they}\end{array}\right)$ fit?

B. I'm afraid (it's/they're) a little too _____.*
Do you have any _____s that are a little _____er?*

A. Yes, we do. I think you'll like (THIS/THESE) _____.
(It's/They're) a little _____er than the one(s) you just **tried on**.

B. Will you **take** (it/them) **back** if I decide to return (it/them)?

A. Of course. No problem at all. Just **bring** (it/them) **back** within _____
days, and we'll **give** you your money **back**.

B. Fine. I think I'll take (it/them). How much $\left(\begin{array}{l}\text{does it}\\\text{do they}\end{array}\right)$ cost?

A. The usual price is _____ dollars. But you're in luck!
We're having a sale this week, and all of our _____s are _____ percent off
the regular price.

B. That's a real bargain! I'm glad I decided to buy (a) _____ this week.
Thank you so much for your help.

A. It's been my pleasure. Please come again.

*
large	–	small
long	–	short
wide	–	narrow
tight	–	loose (baggy)

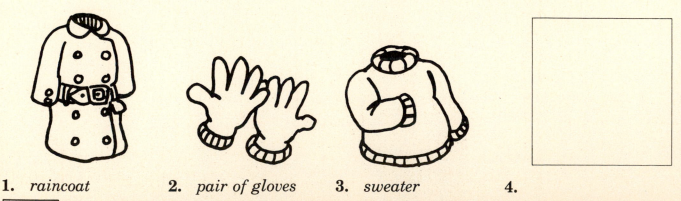

1. *raincoat*   **2.** *pair of gloves*   **3.** *sweater*   **4.**

Connectors:
And ... Too
And ... Either
So, But, Neither

A. I'm hungry.
B. { I am, too. }
   { So am I. }

A. I can swim.
B. { I can, too. }
   { So can I. }

A. I have a car.
B. { I do, too. }
   { So do I. }

A. I worked yesterday.
B. { I did, too. }
   { So did I. }

A. I've seen that movie.
B. { I have, too. }
   { So have I. }

A. I'm not hungry.
B. { I'm not either. }
   { Neither am I. }

A. I can't swim.
B. { I can't either. }
   { Neither can I. }

A. I don't have a car.
B. { I don't either. }
   { Neither do I. }

A. I didn't work yesterday.
B. { I didn't either. }
   { Neither did I. }

A. I haven't seen that movie.
B. { I haven't either. }
   { Neither have I. }

Read and practice.

A. I'm allergic to cats.

B. What a coincidence!
   { I am, too. }
   { So am I. }

A. I wasn't very athletic when I was younger.

B. What a coincidence!
   { I wasn't either. }
   { Neither was I. }

1. I'm a vegetarian.

2. I didn't see the stop sign.

3. I like strawberry ice cream.

4. I don't like war movies.

5. I can speak four languages fluently.

6. I just lost my job.

7. I'm not a very good tennis player.

8. I'll be on vacation next week.

9. I can't sing very well.

10. I've been feeling tired lately.

11. I have to work late at the office tonight.

12. I won't be able to go bowling next Monday night.

13. I don't drink coffee any more.

14. I forgot to take my clothes off the clothes line this morning.

15. I've never kissed anyone before.

16. I'm a little nervous about this operation.

17. I haven't prepared for today's lesson.

18.

I'm tired, { and he is, too. / and so is he. }

He was angry, { and they were, too. / and so were they. }

They work hard, { and she does, too. / and so does she. }

She studied yesterday, { and I did, too. / and so did I. }

A. Why can't you or the children help me with the dishes?

B. I have to study, { **and they do, too.** / **and so do they.** }

1. **A.** Why are you and your brother so tired?
   B. I stayed up late last night, _____.

2. **A.** What are you and your girlfriend going to do tomorrow?
   B. I'm going to study at the library,
   _____.

3. **A.** Why are you and Gloria so nervous?
   B. She has an English exam tomorrow, _____.

4. **A.** Where were you and your husband when the accident happened?
   B. I was standing on the corner,
   _____.

5. **A.** Why can't you or Dr. Johnson see me next Monday?
B. I'll be out of town, _____.

6. **A.** Why haven't you and your sister been in school for the past few days?
B. I've been sick, _____.

7. **A.** How do you know Mr. and Mrs. Jenkins?
B. They sing in the church choir, _____.

8. **A.** Could you or your friend help me bring these packages upstairs?
B. I'll be glad to help you, _____.

9. **A.** Why don't you or your neighbors complain about this broken door?
B. I've already spoken to the landlord, _____.

10. **A.** How did you meet your wife?
B. I was washing clothes at the laundromat one day, _____.

11. **A.** Why are you and your cats hiding under the bed?
B. I'm afraid of thunder and lightning, _____.

12. **A.** What are you two arguing about?
B. He wants this parking space, _____.

13. **A.** Why are you and Peter so angry at each other?
B. I wore a Superman costume to the masquerade party, _____.

14. **A.** Why are you in love with Robert?
B. I appreciate literature, music, and other beautiful things, _____.

I'm not tired, { and he isn't either. / and neither is he. }

He wasn't angry, { and they weren't either. / and neither were they. }

They don't work hard, { and she doesn't either. / and neither does she. }

She didn't study yesterday, { and I didn't either. / and neither did I. }

A. Why do you and your husband want to enroll in my dance class?

B. I can't dance the cha cha or the fox trot,
{ **and he can't either.** / **and neither can he.** }

1. A. Why do you and William look so confused?
   B. I don't understand today's grammar, _____.

2. A. Why didn't you or your parents answer the telephone all weekend?
   B. I wasn't home, _____.

3. A. Why do you and your roommate have to move?
   B. He didn't have enough money to pay the rent this month, _____.

4. A. Why do you and your sister look so frightened?
   B. I've never been on a roller coaster before, _____.

5. **A.** Why are you and your friends so late?
B. I couldn't remember your address, _____.

6. **A.** What do you and Fred want to talk to me about?
B. I won't be able to come to work tomorrow, _____.

7. **A.** Why don't you and your friends want to come to the ballgame?
B. They aren't very interested in baseball, _____.

8. **A.** Why does the school nurse want to see us?
B. I haven't had a flu shot yet, _____.

9. **A.** What are you and your sister arguing about?
B. She doesn't want to take the garbage out, _____.

10. **A.** Why didn't you or Mom wake us up on time this morning?
B. I didn't hear the alarm clock, _____.

11. **A.** Why are you and your husband so quiet this evening?
B. I'm not very comfortable at big parties, _____.

12. **A.** Why were you and your wife so nervous during the flight?
B. I had never flown before today, _____.

13. **A.** Why have you and your friends stopped shopping at my store?
B. I can't afford your prices, _____.

14. **A.** Why don't you and your little sister want me to read *Little Red Riding Hood*?
B. I don't like fairy tales very much, _____.

> I don't sing, but my sister does.
> He can play chess, but I can't.
> We're ready, but they aren't.
> She didn't know the answer, but I did.

A. Do you know the answer to question number 9?

B. No I don't, but **Charles** does. Why don't you ask him?

1. Do you have a hammer?
my upstairs neighbors

2. Are you interested in seeing a movie tonight?
Bob

3. Can you baby-sit for us tomorrow night?
my sister

4. Have you heard tomorrow's weather forecast?
my father

5. Did you write down the homework assignment?
Maria

6. Do you want to go dancing tonight?
Julia

7. Have you by any chance found a brown and white dog?
the people across the street

8. Were you paying attention when the salesman explained how to put together this toy?
the children

Read and practice.

MY BROTHER AND I

In many ways, my brother and I are exactly the same:
    I'm tall and thin, and he is, too.
    I have brown eyes and black curly hair, and so does he.
    I work in an office downtown, and he does, too.
    I'm not married yet, and neither is he.
    I went to college in Boston, and so did he.
    I wasn't a very good student, and he wasn't either.

And in many ways, my brother and I are very different:
    I like classical music, but he doesn't.
    He enjoys sports, but I don't.
    I've never traveled overseas, but he has.
    He's never been to New York, but I have many times.
    He's very outgoing and popular, but I'm not.
    I'm very quiet and philosophical, but he isn't.

Yes, in many ways, my brother and I are exactly the same.
And in many ways, we're very different. But most important of all,
we like and respect each other.   And we're friends.

ON YOUR OWN

Compare yourself with somebody you are close to: a friend,
a classmate, or somebody in your family.

In many ways, _____ and I are exactly the same:
_____
_____
_____

And in many ways, _____ and I are very different:
_____
_____
_____

Passive Voice

> Jim took this photograph.
> This photograph **was taken** by Jim.

Read and practice.

A. This is really a good photograph of you.

B. I think so, too.

A. Who **took** it?

B. I'm not sure. I think it **was taken** by my Uncle George.

A. This is a very sad poem.

B. I think so, too.

A. Who **wrote** it?

B. I'm not sure. I think it **was written** by Shakespeare.

1. This is a very cute photograph of your children.
take

2. This is an excellent magazine article.
write

3. This is a beautiful sonata.
compose

4. This is really an exciting movie.
direct

5. This is a very funny political cartoon.
draw

6. This is a very fine portrait of you.
paint

7. This is a very useful machine.
invent

8. This is an impressive bridge.
build

9. This is a magnificent building.
design

10. This is a very talented elephant.
train

11. This is a very strange computer.
program

12. This is really a crazy fad.
begin

Somebody has fed the cat.
The cat **has been fed**.

Somebody has turned off the lights.
The lights **have been turned off**.

A. Do you want me to feed Rover?

B. No. Don't worry about it.
He's already **been fed**.

A. Do you want me to ring* the church bells?

B. No. Don't worry about it.
They've already **been rung**.

*ring–rang–rung

1. *make the bed*

2. *send the packages*

3. *do the dishes*

4. *sweep the porch*

5. *carve the turkey*

6. *hide*the Christmas presents*

7. *write down Mary's telephone number*

8. *freeze† the leftover chicken*

9. *take the garbage out*

10. *wake‡ the children up*

11. *teach two-word verbs today*

12. *sing the National Anthem*

*hide–hid–hidden
†freeze–froze–frozen
‡wake–woke–woken

A. Have you heard about Harry?

B. No, I haven't. What happened?

A. He **was fired** last week.

B. What a shame!*
That's the second time he**'s been fired** this year!

A. Have you heard about Helen?

B. No, I haven't. What happened?

A. She **was given** a raise last week.

B. That's great!†
That's the second time she**'s been given** a raise this year!

*You can also say: That's terrible!   That's too bad!
†You can also say: That's fantastic!   That's wonderful!

1. *Mr. and Mrs. Wilson
robbed*

2. *Uncle John
invited to the White House*

3. *Larry*
hurt in a car accident

4. *Maria*
promoted

5. *our mailman*
bitten* by a dog

6. *the man across the street*
arrested

7. *Claudia*
sent to Honolulu on business

8. *Mrs. Miller*
taken to the hospital by ambulance

9. *Arthur*
rejected by the army

10. *Lana*
offered a movie contract

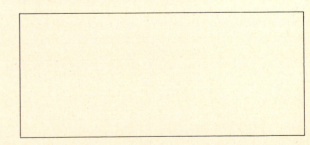

11. *Walter*
chosen† "employee of the month"

12.

*bite–bit–bitten
†choose–chose–chosen

Somebody is repairing my car.
My car is **being repaired**.

A. Hello. Is this Joe's Auto Repair Shop?

B. Yes, it is. Can I help you?

A. Yes, please. This is Mrs. Jones.
I'm calling about my car.
Has it **been repaired** yet?

B. Not yet. It's **being repaired** right now.

A. Can I pick it up soon?

B. Yes. Come by at four o'clock.
I'm sure it'll be ready by then.

A. Hello. Is this _____'s _____?

B. Yes, it is. Can I help you?

A. Yes, please. This is _____.
I'm calling about my _____.
(Has it/Have they) been _____ yet?

B. Not yet. (It's/They're) being _____ right now.

A. Can I pick (it/them) up soon?

B. Yes. Come by at _____ o'clock.
I'm sure (it'll/they'll) be ready by then.

1. *watch*
repair

2. *TV*
fix

3. *pants*
take in

4. *poodle*
clip

5. *will*
rewrite

6.

> Answers **should be written** in your notebook.
> Students **should be required** to take an examination.
> Smoking **shouldn't be allowed** in the classroom.

WHAT'S YOUR OPINION?

Talk about these issues with other students in your class.

1. **Should** your native language **be spoken** during the English class?

2. **Should** students **be allowed** to use dictionaries during the language lesson?

3. When **should** young people **be allowed** to drive?
   drink?
   vote?
   go out on dates by themselves?

4. **Should** smoking **be permitted** in public places?

5. **Should** everybody (men and women) **be required** to serve in the army?

Noun/Adjective/Adverb Review:

Count/Non-Count Nouns
Comparative of Adjectives
Superlative of Adjectives
Comparative of Adverbs

many a few	much a little
paper clips eggs mushrooms · · ·	sugar paper toothpaste · · ·

Read and practice.

A. Could I possibly borrow some paper clips?*

B. Sure. **How many** do you need?

A. Just **a few**.

B. Here! Take **as many as** you want!

A. Thank you very much.

B. You're welcome.

A. Could I possibly borrow some sugar?*

B. Sure. **How much** do you need?

A. Just **a little.**

B. Here! Take **as much as** you want!

A. Thank you very much.

B. You're welcome.

*You can also say:
Could you possibly lend me some paper clips/sugar?
Could you possibly spare some paper clips/sugar?

1. *rubber bands*

2. *typing paper*

104

3. *eggs*

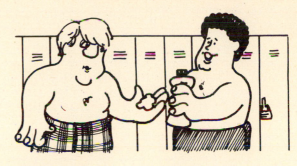

4. *shampoo*

5. *flour*

6. *envelopes*

7. *ink*

8. *mushrooms*

9. *laundry detergent*

10. *toothpaste*

11. *one-dollar bills*

12.

cheap – cheaper	interesting – more interesting
nice – nicer	beautiful – more beautiful
big – bigger	honest – more honest
friendly – friendlier	reliable – more reliable

A. I need some advice.
I can't decide whether I should **buy a used car or a new car**.
What do you think?

B. Hmm. That's a difficult question.
Used cars are **cheaper** than new cars.
On the other hand, new cars are **more reliable** than used cars.
I really don't know what to tell you.

friendly   clean   intelligent   nice

1. *buy a dog or a cat*   **2.** *go out on a date with Ted or Ronald*

3. *study English with Miss Jones or Mrs. Green*

4. *buy ice cream or yogurt for dessert this evening*

5. *go to the supermarket across the street or the supermarket around the corner*

6. *buy a motorcycle or a bicycle*

7. *hire Mr. Clark or Mr. Davis*

8. *vote for Timothy White or Edward Pratt*

9. *take my girlfriend to a discotheque or a cafe tonight*

10.

warm	–	warmer	–	the warmest
friendly	–	friendlier	–	the friendliest
nice	–	nicer	–	the nicest
big	–	bigger	–	the biggest
interesting	–	more interesting	–	the most interesting
comfortable	–	more comfortable	–	the most comfortable
patient	–	more patient	–	the most patient

A. How do you like your new apartment?

B. I like it very much. It's really **big**.

A. Is it **bigger** than your old apartment?

B. It sure is!
It's **the biggest** apartment I've ever had.

A. How do you like your new English teacher?

B. I like him very much. He's really **patient**.

A. Is he **more patient** than your old English teacher?

B. He sure is!
He's **the most patient** English teacher I've ever had.

1. *winter coat*
   warm

2. *dance teacher*
   talented

3. *boss*
nice

4. *job*
interesting

5. *armchair*
comfortable

6. *bicycle*
fast

7. *briefcase*
sturdy

8. *vacuum cleaner*
powerful

9. *dentist*
good*

10. *roommate*
considerate

11. *parrot*
talkative

12.

*good–better–best

gracefully – more gracefully accurately – more accurately carefully – more carefully	fast – faster
	well – better

A. I think I'm getting old.

B. Why do you say that?

A. I don't **dance** as **gracefully** as I used to.

B. That's not true!
You **dance more gracefully** than anybody I know.

A. You're just saying that!

B. No. I really mean it.

1. *drive*
carefully

2. *type*
accurately

3. *sing beautifully*

4. *write neatly*

5. *play tennis well*

6. *jog fast*

7. *think clearly*

8. *work energetically*

9. *play baseball well*

10. *look at life enthusiastically*

11. *speak Russian fluently*

12.

TV COMMERCIALS

Read and practice this commercial.

A. I've been worried about my **kitchen floor** recently.

B. Really? What's the matter with your **kitchen floor**?

A. It isn't **shiny** enough, and I don't know how to make it **shinier**.
Do you have any ideas?

B. Yes, I do.
Have you ever tried PRESTO FLOOR WAX?

A. No, I haven't.
Does it make **kitchen floors shinier**?

B. It sure does!
I remember when I was worried about MY **kitchen floor**.
It wasn't as **shiny** as I wanted it to be.
But one day somebody told me about PRESTO FLOOR WAX.
I started using it, and now everybody tells me I have **the shiniest kitchen floor** in town!

A. Thanks for the advice.
I think I'll go to a store and get some right away.

B. You won't regret it.

Using the script above as a guide, prepare commercials for these products with other students in your class.

1. *windows clean*   **2.** *hair attractive*   **3.** *teeth white*   **4.**

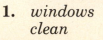

Embedded Questions

Where is the bank?	I don't know where the bank is.
What is he doing?	I don't know what he's doing.
Why were they crying?	I don't know why they were crying.
When can he visit us?	I don't know when he can visit us.

Read and practice.

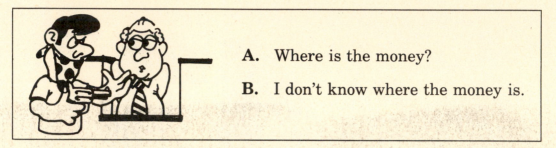

A. Where is the money?

B. I don't know where the money is.

Ask and answer these questions using one of the following expressions in your answer:

I don't know . . ., I don't remember . . ., I can't remember . . ., I've forgotten . . ., I'm not sure . . ., I have no idea . . .

1. Where are my keys?

2. What was his license number?

3. What are they arguing about?

4. When will the train arrive?

5. Who should I call?

6. Who was the eleventh president of the United States?

7. How long have Mr. and Mrs. Appleton been married?

8. How long has Alan been working here?

9. When is Santa Claus going to come?

Where does he live?   I don't know where he lives.
How often do they come here?   I don't know how often they come here.
How did she break her leg?   I don't know how she broke her leg.

A. What did the robber look like?

B. I don't remember what he looked like.

I don't know . . ., I don't remember . . ., I can't remember . . ., I've forgotten . . ., I'm not sure . . ., I have no idea . . .

1. Where did you buy your winter coat?

2. How much do eggs cost this week?

3. How often does the ice cream truck come by?

4. What time does the movie begin?

5. When did Mom and Dad get married?

6. What did we do in English class yesterday?

7. Why do young people like such loud music?

8. When did you decide to become a teacher?

9. How much does a haircut cost these days?

Where is the bank?	
Do you know	
Can you tell me	
Could you tell me	
Could you please tell me	where the bank is?
Could you possibly tell me	
Do you have any idea	
Do you by any chance know	

A. Do you know what time the concert begins?

B. I'm sorry. I don't know. You should ask the man at the box office. He can tell you what time the concert begins.

A. Can you tell me how long I've been here?

B. I'm sorry. I don't know. You should ask your nurse. She can tell you how long you've been here.

1. *Do you know . . .*
ask the ticket agent

2. *Do you by any chance know . . .*
ask the people next door

3. *Could you please tell me . . .*
ask the teacher

4. *Do you by any chance know . . .*
talk to the salesman

5. *Can you tell me . . .*
check with the mechanic

6. *Do you know . . .*
call her friend Patty

7. *Can you tell me . . .*
ask your older brother

8. *Do you know . . .*
ask that policeman over there

9. *Do you have any idea . . .*
call the superintendent

10. *Do you know . . .*
ask his supervisor

11. *Do you by any chance know . . .*
ask the boss

12.

Is Tom in school today?

Do you know { if / whether } Tom is in school today?

I don't know { if / whether } Tom is in school today.

Does Mary work here?

Do you know { if / whether } Mary works here?

I don't know { if / whether } Mary works here.

A. Do you know { if / whether } honey is bad for my teeth?

B. I'm not really sure. Why don't you ask your dentist?

He can tell you { if / whether } honey is bad for your teeth.

A. Can you tell me { if / whether } anybody here found a black wallet?

B. I'm not really sure. Why don't you ask the manager?

She can tell you { if / whether } anybody here found a black wallet.

1. *Can you tell me . . .*
ask the doctor

2. *Do you know . . .*
speak to the stewardess

3. *Do you know . . .*
ask Mom

4. *Could you possibly tell me . . .*
check with the ticket agent

5. *Do you by any chance know . . .*
speak to the teacher

6. *Could you please tell me . . .*
ask the bus driver

7. *Can you tell me . . .*
ask the librarian

8. *Do you know . . .*
ask the music teacher

9. *Can you tell me . . .*
check with the woman at the box office

10. *Do you know . . .*
call the landlord

11. *Can you tell me . . .*
ask those people over there

12.

I WANT TO REPORT A MISSING PERSON!

<u>Police Department</u>
<u>Missing Persons Information Sheet</u>

1. What is your name?

2. What is the missing person's name?

3. What is his/her address?

4. How old is he/she?

5. How tall is he/she?

6. How much does he/she weigh?

7. Does this person have any scars, birthmarks, or other special characteristics?

8. Where was he/she the last time you saw him/her?

9. What was he/she wearing at that time?

10. What was he/she doing?

11. What is your relationship to the missing person?

12. What is your telephone number?

13. When can we reach you at that number?

A student in your class is missing! Call the police!

3. Can you tell me . . .

4. Do you know . . .

5. Can you tell me . . .

6. Do you have any idea . . .

7. Do you by any chance know . . .

8. Can you tell me . . .

9. Could you possibly tell me . . .

10. And can you tell me . . .

11. Would you please tell me . . .

12. Can you tell me . . .

13. Could you possibly tell me . . .

14

Perfect Modals:
   Should Have
   Must Have
   Might Have
   May Have
   Could Have

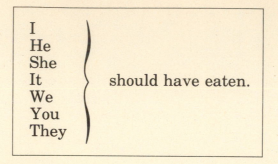

I	
He	
She	
It	should have eaten.
We	
You	
They	

Read and practice.

A. Did Richard speak loud enough in the school play last night?

B. No, he didn't.
He **should have spoken** louder.

1. Did Bob drive carefully enough during his driving test?
more carefully

2. Did Lucy study hard enough for her English exam?
harder

3. Did Theodore practice long enough for his piano lesson?
longer

4. Did Mr. and Mrs. Gleason get to the airport early enough?
earlier

5. Did Mr. Franklin write legibly enough on his income tax form?
more legibly

6. Did Harriet take her chocolate cake out of the oven soon enough?
sooner

7. Did Mr. Johnson dress comfortably enough at the beach?
more comfortably

8. Did Sally speak confidently enough at her job interview?
more confidently

| I |
| He |
| She |
| It | } must have eaten.
| We |
| You |
| They |

A. Mr. Jones came to work late today.

B. I'm really surprised to hear that. Mr. Jones NEVER comes to work late!

A. I know. He **must have overslept.**

1. Sherman went to the doctor yesterday.
feel very bad

2. Beverly smoked two packs of cigarettes yesterday.
be very nervous

3. The students in my English class made lots of mistakes today.
have trouble with the lesson

4. Mr. Crabapple smiled at his employees this morning.
be in a very good mood

5. Judy refused to eat her dinner last night.
eat too many cookies after school

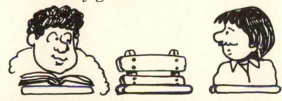

6. Maria missed English class all last week.
be very sick

7. You talked in your sleep last night.
have a bad dream

8. Walter was in a terrible mood today.
"get up on the wrong side of the bed"

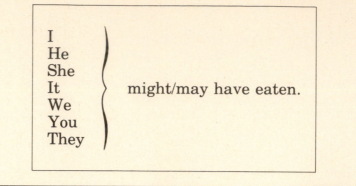

| I |
| He |
| She |
| It | might/may have eaten. |
| We |
| You |
| They |

A. Why does John look so tired?

B. He **must have swum fifty laps** today.

A. I'm not so sure.   He $\left\{\begin{array}{l}\textbf{MIGHT}\\\textbf{MAY}\end{array}\right\}$ **have swum fifty laps,**
but **swimming fifty laps** doesn't usually make him so tired.

B. I'm a little concerned.   Maybe we should talk with him.

A. That's a good idea.

A. Why does Barbara look so upset?

B. She **must have failed an exam** today.

A. I'm not so sure.   She $\left\{\begin{array}{l}\textbf{MIGHT}\\\textbf{MAY}\end{array}\right\}$ **have failed an exam,**
but **failing an exam** doesn't usually make her so upset.

B. I'm a little concerned.   Maybe we should talk with her.

A. That's a good idea.

1. Why does Martha look so nervous?
drink* too much coffee

2. Why does Fred look so tired?
work overtime

3. Why does Peggy look so exhausted?
jog a little too much

4. Why does Peter look so upset?
argue with the boss

5. Why does Senator Johnson
look so tired?
shake† a lot of hands

6. Why does Roger look so upset?
have a fight with his girlfriend

7. Why does our English teacher
look so angry?
*find a lot of mistakes
in our homework*

8. Why does our cat look so scared?
*be chased by the dog
across the street*

*drink–drank–drunk
†shake–shook–shaken

<table>
<tr><td>I
He
She
It
We
You
They</td><td>could have eaten.</td></tr>
</table>

A. You won't believe what George did yesterday!

B. What did he do?

A. He moved his piano by himself.

B. You're kidding!
He shouldn't have moved his piano by himself.

A. Of course he shouldn't have. He {could / might} have broken his back!

1. *go hiking by himself in the mountains*
get lost

2. *eat all the ice cream in the refrigerator*
get sick

3. *go skating on the town pond*
fall* through the ice

4. *play baseball in the rain*
catch a bad cold

*fall–fell–fallen

5. *ride her bicycle downtown*
get hurt

6. *swim to the other side of the lake*
drown

7. *try to fix their TV by themselves*
be electrocuted

8. *shout back at the boss*
get fired

9. *run in the Boston Marathon*
have a heart attack

10. *mix nitric acid and glycerin*
blow* up the school

11. *get into an argument with*
a policeman
wind up in jail

12.

*blow–blew–blown

Read and practice.

I OWE YOU AN APOLOGY

A. I owe you an apology.

B. What for?

A. You must have been very angry with me yesterday.

B. I don't understand. Why should I have been angry with you?

A. Don't you remember?
We had planned to **see a movie** yesterday, but I completely forgot!

B. Don't worry about it.
In fact, I owe YOU an apology.

A. You do? Why?

B. I couldn't have **seen a movie** with you anyway. I had to **take care of my little sister** yesterday . . . and I completely forgot to tell you.

A. That's O.K. Maybe we can **see a movie** some time soon.

A. I owe you an apology.

B. What for?

A. You must have been very angry with me yesterday.

B. I don't understand.   Why should I have been angry with you?

A. Don't you remember?
We had planned to _____ yesterday, but I completely forgot!

B. Don't worry about it.
In fact, I owe YOU an apology.

A. You do?   Why?

B. I couldn't have _____ with you anyway.
I had to _____ yesterday . . . and I completely forgot to tell you.

A. That's O.K.   Maybe we can _____ some time soon.

1. *play tennis*
go to the doctor

2. *go swimming*
visit a friend in the hospital

3. *have lunch*
go to an important meeting

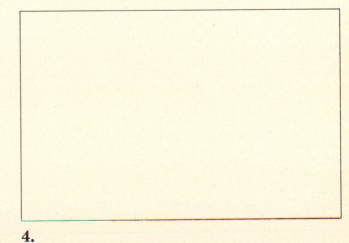

4.

Conditional:
Present Real
(If ____ Will)
Present Unreal
(If ____ Would)
Hope-Clauses

Read and practice.

A. What are you going to do this weekend?

B. We aren't sure.
If the weather is good, we'll probably go to the beach.
If the weather is bad, we'll probably stay home.

1. How is Tom going to get to work
      tomorrow?

He isn't sure.
If it rains, _____.
If it's sunny, _____.

2. What are Mr. and Mrs. Green
      going to do tonight?

They aren't sure.
If they're tired, _____.
If they have some energy, _____.

3. Where are you going to have lunch
      today?

I'm not sure.
If I'm in a hurry, _____.
If I have some time, _____.

4. What's Jane going to do tomorrow?

She isn't sure.
If she still has a cold, _____.
If she feels better, _____.

5. Where is Patty going to go after school
      today?

She isn't sure.
If she has a lot of homework, _____.
If she doesn't have a lot of homework,

_____.

6. What's Henry going to have
      for dessert this evening?

He isn't sure.
If he decides to stay on his diet, _____.
If he decides to forget about his diet,

_____.

A. Do you think Johnny should go to school today?

B. No, I don't.
If Johnny goes to school today, he might **give his cold to the other children**.

1. Do you think I should put some more salt in the soup?
spoil it

2. Do you think I should skip English class today?
miss something important

3. Do you think Rover should come to the beach with us?
get carsick

4. Do you think I should try to break up that fight?
get hurt

5. Do you think Mary should quit her job?
have trouble finding another one

6. Do you think Teddy should stay up and watch TV with us?
have trouble getting up in the morning

7. Do you think I should marry Norman?
regret it for the rest of your life

8.

I hope it rains tomorrow.
I hope it doesn't rain tomorrow.

A. Do you think it'll be a hot summer?

B. I hope not.
If **it's a hot summer**, our classroom will be very warm.
And if **our classroom is very warm**, it'll be impossible to study English!

A. You're right. I hope **it isn't a hot summer**.

1.

A. Do you think the train will be very crowded?

B. I hope not.
If _____, we'll have to stand.
And if _____, we'll be exhausted by the time we get to work!

A. You're right. I hope _____.

2.

A. Do you think the boss will retire this year?

B. I hope not.
If _____, his son will take his place.
And if _____, everybody will quit!

A. You're right. I hope _____.

3.

A. Do you think it'll be very cold tonight?

B. I hope not.
If _____, our car won't start in the morning.
And if _____, we'll have to walk to work!

A. You're right. I hope _____.

4.

A. Do you think our mathematics teacher will give us an exam tomorrow?

B. I hope not.
If _____, we'll get bad grades.
And if _____, our parents will be very upset!

A. You're right. I hope _____.

5.

A. Do you think it'll rain tomorrow?

B. I hope not.
If _____, we'll have to cancel the school picnic.
And if _____, everybody will be very disappointed!

A. You're right. I hope _____.

6.

A. Do you think the bus will be late today?

B. I hope not.
If _____, we won't get to work on time.
And if _____, the boss will be very angry!

A. You're right. I hope _____.

7.

A. Do you think inflation will get worse this year?

B. I hope not.
If _____, I'll have to take a second job.
And if _____, my family will be very upset!

A. You're right. I hope _____.

8.

A. Do you think our landlord will raise the rent this year?

B. I hope not.
If _____, we won't be able to pay it.
And if _____, we'll have to move!

A. You're right. I hope _____.

9.

A. Do you think our TV will be at the repair shop for a long time?

B. I hope not.
If _____, we won't have anything to do in the evening.
And if _____, we'll go crazy!

A. You're right. I hope _____.

I	would		I'd	
He	would		He'd	
She	would		She'd	
It	would	→		work.
We	would		We'd	
You	would		You'd	
They	would		They'd	

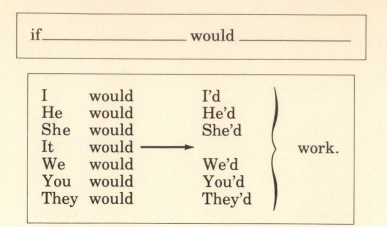

A. Why don't our grandchildren visit us more often?

B. They don't have enough time.
If they had more time, they'd visit us more often.

A. Why isn't Melvin a good salesman?

B. He isn't aggressive enough.
If he were* more aggressive, he'd be a good salesman.

*If [I, he, she, it, we, you, they] were . . .

1. A. Why doesn't Sally get good grades?
B. She doesn't study enough.
If_____.

2. A. Why isn't Mark a good driver?
B. He isn't careful enough.
If_____.

3. **A.** Why don't I feel energetic?
   B. You don't sleep enough.
   If_____.

4. **A.** Why doesn't Alexander enjoy playing baseball?
   B. He isn't athletic enough.
   If_____.

5. **A.** Why doesn't Julie have friends at school?
   B. She isn't outgoing enough.
   If_____.

6. **A.** Why doesn't Sidney have a yearly checkup?
   B. He isn't concerned enough about his health.
   If_____.

7. **A.** Why aren't you satisfied with your jobs?
   B. We don't get paid enough.
   If_____.

8. **A.** Why don't I enjoy life?
   B. You aren't relaxed enough.
   If_____.

9. **A.** Why aren't most Americans in good physical condition?
   B. They don't exercise enough.
   If_____.

10. **A.** Why don't Tom and Janet get along with each other?
    B. They don't have enough in common.
    If_____.

11. **A.** Why don't our congressmen do something about pollution?
    B. They aren't concerned enough about the environment.
    If_____.

12. **A.** Why doesn't our English teacher buy a new pair of shoes?
    B. He doesn't make enough money.
    If_____.

A. I wonder why Fred works so hard.

B. I don't know.   He must like his job.

A. You're probably right.
If he didn't like his job, he wouldn't work so hard.

A. I wonder why my older brother and his girlfriend hold hands all the time.

B. I don't know.   They must be in love.

A. You're probably right.
If they weren't in love, they wouldn't hold hands all the time.

1. I wonder why Barbara wants to be a
schoolteacher.
She must like children.

2. I wonder why Alan makes
so many mistakes.
He must be careless.

3. I wonder why Nancy is so nervous.
She must have an exam today.

4. I wonder why our teacher is shouting at us today.
She must be in a bad mood.

5. I wonder why Rover is barking at the door.
He must want to go outside.

6. I wonder why Bob is so dressed up today.
He must be going to a job interview.

7. I wonder why John gets into so many fights.
He must like to argue with people.

8. I wonder why Judy wants a telescope for her birthday.
She must be interested in astronomy.

9. I wonder why Jeff is home tonight.
He must have to take care of his little brother.

10. I wonder why Shirley goes hiking in the mountains every weekend.
She must enjoy nature.

11. I wonder why I'm sneezing so much.
You must be allergic to my perfume.

12.

ARE YOU PREPARED FOR EMERGENCIES?

Answer these questions and ask other students in your class.

1. What would you do if you saw someone choking on a piece of food?

2. What would you do if you saw someone having a heart attack?

3. What would you do if you were at the beach and you saw someone drowning?

4. What would you do if somebody in your family were missing?

5. What would you do if somebody came up to you on the street and tried to rob you?

6. What would you do if a fire broke out in your house or apartment?

7. What would you do if you were lying in bed and you heard someone trying to break into your house or apartment?

8. What would you do if you were bitten by a dog?

Think of some other emergencies and ask other students if they're prepared:

_____

_____

_____

Present Unreal Conditional
(continued)
Wish-Clauses

Read and practice.

A. Do you think the boss would be angry if I went home early?

B. Of course he would.   He'd be VERY angry.

A. Do you really think so?

B. I'm positive.*
I wouldn't go home early if I were you.

A. I suppose you're right.

*You can also say: Without a doubt.   There's no question in my mind.

1. Do you think Roger would be disappointed if I missed his birthday party?

2. Do you think our English teacher would be upset if I skipped class tomorrow?

3. Do you think Mom and Dad would be angry if I borrowed the car?

4. Do you think our neighbors would be annoyed if I turned on the stereo?

5. Do you think Jack would be jealous if I took out his girlfriend?

6. Do you think the voters would be upset if I raised taxes?

7. Do you think Jennifer would be mad if I rode her bicycle?

8. Do you think the landlord would be upset if I painted the kitchen purple?

9. Do you think my parents would be disappointed if I dropped out of school?

10. Do you think my fans would be unhappy if I got a haircut?

11. Do you think Tom would be embarrassed if I showed his girlfriend a photograph of him in the bathtub when he was two years old?

12.

> Tom **lives** in Boston.　He **wishes** he **lived** in New York.

A. Do you enjoy driving a school bus?

B. Not really.
I wish I drove a taxi.

A. Does Mr. Robinson enjoy being a teacher?

B. Not really.
He wishes he were an actor.

1. Does Mary enjoy living in the suburbs?
in the city

2. Does Mrs. Kramer enjoy teaching math?
something else

3. Does Larry enjoy being single?
married

4. Do you enjoy working here?
someplace else

5. Does Ralph enjoy selling used cars?
insurance

6. Does Oscar enjoy painting houses?
portraits

7. Do you enjoy being the vice-president?
the president

8. Does Sarah enjoy having two part-time jobs?
one good full-time job

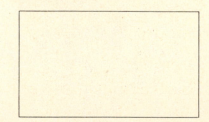

9.

Mary **can** sing.	She **wishes** she **could** dance.

A. Can Jonathan dance?

B. No, he can't . . . but he wishes he could.
If he could dance, he'd **go dancing every night**.

1. Can Mary sew?
make all her own clothes

2. Can Steve quit smoking?
be a lot healthier

3. Can Gloria find her keys?
be able to get into her apartment

4. Can Richard find his glasses?
watch TV tonight

5. Can Janet type fast?
be able to get a better job

6. Can Henry fix his car by himself?
save a lot of money

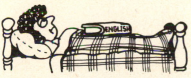

7. Can Maria stop thinking about
tomorrow's English test?
get a good night's sleep

8. Can Ronald play a musical
instrument?
*be able to march
in the school parade*

9. Can Jessica talk?
*tell her parents she doesn't like
her baby food*

10.

$$\text{if} \underline{\hspace{3cm}} \left\{ \begin{array}{l} \text{could} \\ \text{would be able to} \end{array} \right\} \underline{\hspace{3cm}}$$

A. Are you glad that your landlord is going to repaint your apartment this Saturday?

B. No, not really.
To tell the truth, I wish my landlord WEREN'T going to repaint my apartment this Saturday.

A. Why?

B. If my landlord weren't going to repaint my apartment this Saturday, $\left\{ \begin{array}{l} \text{I could} \\ \text{I'd be able to} \end{array} \right\}$ go away for the weekend.

A. Are you pleased that your son wants to be a dentist?

B. No, not really.
To tell the truth, I wish my son DIDN'T want to be a dentist.

A. Why?

B. If my son didn't want to be a dentist, $\left\{ \begin{array}{l} \text{I could} \\ \text{I'd be able to} \end{array} \right\}$ train him to manage my shoe store when I retire.

1. Are you happy that your aunt and uncle are coming to visit tomorrow?
go skiing

2. Are you glad that the weather is going to be nice this weekend?
wear my new raincoat for the first time

3. Are you happy that the boss wants to take you to dinner tomorrow?

go home early

4. Are you glad that the TV is fixed?

talk to the children

5. Are you happy that your daughter is going to a college out of town?

see her more often

6. Are you glad that you live in a high-rise building?

have a garden

7. Are you pleased that your son takes drum lessons?

have some "peace and quiet" around the house

8. Are you happy that your parents are going to have a birthday party for you this Saturday?

go out and celebrate with my friends

9. Are you pleased that your new office has a view of the park?

concentrate more on my work

10. Are you glad that you're studying difficult grammar now?

do my homework in just a few minutes

I NEED SOME ADVICE

Read and practice.

A. Would you mind if I asked you for some advice?

B. Of course I wouldn't mind.

A. I'm thinking of **buying a used car from Ralph Jones**, but I'm not sure that's a very good idea. What do you think?

B. Do you want my honest opinion?

A. Yes, of course.

B. Well . . . to tell the truth, I wouldn't **buy a used car from Ralph Jones** if I were you. If you **bought a used car from Ralph Jones**, you'd probably **regret it**.

A. I guess you're right. Thanks for the advice.

1. *ask the boss for a raise this week*
get fired

2. *grow a moustache*
look very funny

3. *work overtime this weekend*
be exhausted by Monday morning

4.

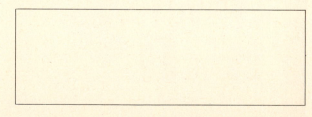

Past Unreal Conditional (If ___ Would Have ___) Wish-Clauses (continued)

if_____would have_____

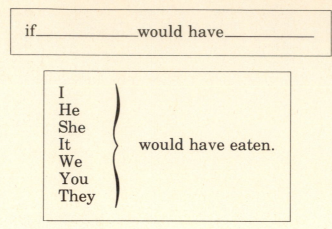

I He She It We You They	would have eaten.

Read and practice.

A. Why didn't Peter take his umbrella to work today?

B. He didn't know it was going to rain.
If he had known it was going to rain, he would have taken his umbrella to work today.

A. Why weren't you in class yesterday?

B. I wasn't feeling well.
If I had been feeling well, I would have been in class yesterday.

1. A. Why didn't you do your homework last night?

B. I didn't bring my book home.
If_____.

2. A. Why wasn't Sally on time for work this morning?

B. Her alarm clock didn't ring.
If_____.

152

3. A. Why didn't you send me a postcard?
B. We didn't remember your address.
If_____.

4. A. Why didn't Mr. and Mrs. Clark watch the President's speech last night?
B. Their TV wasn't working.
If_____.

5. A. Why didn't you come * to the party last night?
B. I wasn't invited.
If_____.

6. A. Why didn't Mrs. Brown's students give her a birthday present?
B. She didn't tell them it was her birthday.
If_____.

7. A. Why didn't you make your beds this morning?
B. We didn't have enough time.
If_____.

8. A. Why didn't you go to the movies with your friends last night?
B. I wasn't in the mood to see a film.
If_____.

9. A. Why didn't Mr. and Mrs. Green enjoy the play last night?
B. They didn't have good seats.
If_____.

10. A. Why wasn't Senator Maxwell re-elected?
B. The people didn't trust him.
If_____.

11. A. Why didn't Harry stop at that traffic light?
B. He wasn't looking.
If_____.

12. A. Why wasn't Sophia asked to sing an encore last night?
B. The audience wasn't pleased with her performance.
If_____.

*come–came–come

A. I wonder why John ran by without saying hello.

B. He must have **been in a hurry**.

A. You're probably right.
If he hadn't been in a hurry, he wouldn't have run by without saying hello.

1. I wonder why Gregory arrived late for work.
miss the bus

2. I wonder why Mario was absent from English class all last week.
be very sick

3. I wonder why Betty quit.
find a better job

4. I wonder why Rover got sick last night.
eat something he shouldn't have

5. I wonder why the apple pie tasted so fresh.

be baked this morning

6. I wonder why Mom went to sleep so early.

have a hard day at the office

7. I wonder why Helen prepared so much food.

expect a lot of people to come to her party

8. I wonder why the boss was so irritable today.

be upset about something

9. I wonder why my cactus plant died.

have a rare disease

10. I wonder why Eleanor went home early today.

be feeling "under the weather"

11. I wonder why Dad got stopped by a policeman.

be driving too fast

12. I wonder why my barber cut my hair so quickly today.

have a lot of customers after you

13. I wonder why my shirt shrank* so much.

be 100 percent cotton

14.

*shrink–shrank–shrunk

| Tom **lives** in Boston. He **wishes** he **lived** in New York. | Tom **lived** in Boston. He **wishes** he **had lived** in New York. |

A. Does Albert know his neighbors?

B. No, he doesn't.
But he WISHES he **knew his neighbors**.
If he knew his neighbors, he wouldn't **be so lonely**.

A. Did Linda know how to get around the city when she moved here?

B. No, she didn't.
But she WISHES she **had known how to get around the city.**
If she had known how to get around the city, she wouldn't have **been so confused.**

1. Does Donald have a good memory?
forget people's names all the time

2. Did Sharon have her shopping list with her this morning?
forget* to buy eggs

***forget–forgot–forgotten**

3. Does Judy drive to work?
have to wait for the bus every morning

4. Did you drive to work today?
have to wait forty minutes for the subway

5. Does Paul have a good job?
be so concerned about his future

6. Did you have a flu shot last fall?
be sick all winter

7. Does Brenda do daily exercises?
have to go on a diet

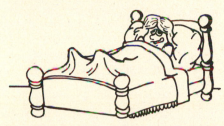

8. Did Ivan do his homework last night?
have to do his homework early this morning

9. Is Philip an optimist?
get depressed so often

10. Was Alice prepared for her English test?
get a low grade

11. Do Mr. and Mrs. Taylor take dance lessons?
feel so "out of place" at discotheques

12. Did Harry take two aspirin when his tooth began to hurt?
feel so much pain

WISHES AND HOPES

I hope it's sunny tomorrow.	(It might be sunny.)
I wish it were sunny.	(It isn't sunny.)
I wish it had been sunny during our picnic.	(It wasn't sunny.)

Read and practice.

1.

A. I hope it's a nice day tomorrow.

B. How come?

A. If it's a nice day tomorrow, we'll be able to go to the beach.

2.

A. I wish I were taller.

B. Why?

A. If I were taller, I'd be able to reach the cookie jar.

3.

A. I wish I had saved my wedding dress.

B. Why?

A. If I had saved my wedding dress, I could have given it to you for your wedding.

4.

A. I wish I had finished medical school.

B. What makes you say that?

A. If I had finished medical school, I probably would have been a very good doctor.

5.

A. I hope we don't have to go to school tomorrow.

B. I hope so, too.

A. If we don't have to go to school tomorrow, we can play outside all day and build a snowman.

6.

A. I wish I didn't have to go to work tomorrow.

B. Why?

A. If I didn't have to go to work tomorrow, I could watch my daughter perform in her school play.

7.

A. I wish we hadn't bought Teddy a chemistry set for his birthday.

B. How come?

A. If we hadn't bought Teddy a chemistry set for his birthday, he wouldn't have set the house on fire.

What do YOU hope? What do YOU wish? Why?
Share your thoughts with other students in your class.

Reported Speech
Sequence of Tenses

He said,	He said (that)*
"I'm sick."	. . . he was sick.
"I like jazz."	. . . he liked jazz.
"I'm going to buy a new car."	. . . he was going to buy a new car.
"I went to Paris last year."	. . . he had gone to Paris last year.
"I've already seen that movie."	. . . he had already seen that movie.
"I was studying."	. . . he had been studying.
"I'll call you tomorrow."	. . . he would call me tomorrow.
"I can help you."	. . . he could help me.

Read and practice.

A. I forgot to tell you. Marvin called yesterday.

B. Really? What did he say?

A. He said (that)* **he thought he was falling in love with me.**

A. I forgot to tell you. _____ called yesterday.

B. Really? What did _____ say?

A. _____ said (that)*_____.

*You can also say: told me (that).

1. *our oldest son*

I'm working very hard at college this year.

2. *the TV repairman*

I can't fix your TV.

3. *our niece Patty*

I got a raise last week.

4. *our nephew Robert*

I've been fired.

5. *Uncle Charlie*

I'll be arriving this Friday on the two o'clock train.

6. *our upstairs neighbors*

We're going to move to a new apartment.

7. *my boss*

You don't have to work overtime next week.

8. *Peggy and George*

We won't be able to come to your party.

9. *Aunt Edith*

I'll send you a postcard from Rome.

10. *my boyfriend*

I'm sorry I forgot about your birthday.

11. *the little girl down the street*

I'll be glad to baby-sit this Saturday night.

12. *the auto mechanic*

The car is ready and you can pick it up any time you want to.

13. *my sister*

I saw you at the shopping mall, but you didn't see me.

14. *Grandma*

I was planning to visit this weekend, but I won't be able to come because I have the flu.

John works here.	I knew I didn't know }	(that) John worked here.

A. What's everybody talking about?

B. Haven't you heard?
Jack is going to be a father!

A. You're kidding! I didn't know (that) Jack was going to be a father.

B. You didn't?! I thought EVERYBODY knew (that) Jack was going to be a father!

A. What's everybody _____ about?

B. Haven't you heard?
_____!

A. You're kidding! I didn't know (that) _____.

B. You didn't?! I thought EVERYBODY knew (that) _____!

1. What's everybody so upset about?

2. What's everybody talking about?

3. What's everybody so happy about?

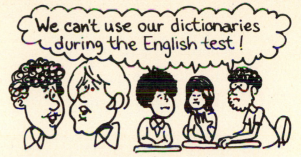

4. What's everybody so upset about?

5. What's everybody so angry about?

6. What's everybody so nervous about?

7. What's everybody so excited about?

8. What's everybody so happy about?

9. What's everybody so excited about?

10. What's everybody talking about?

11. What's everybody so upset about?

12.

He asked,	He asked me
"Where is the bank?"	. . . where the bank was.
"When are you going to visit me?"	. . . when I was going to visit him.
"Do you speak English?"	. . . $\left\{ \begin{array}{c} \text{if} \\ \text{whether} \end{array} \right\}$ I spoke English.
"Have you seen Mary?"	. . . $\left\{ \begin{array}{c} \text{if} \\ \text{whether} \end{array} \right\}$ I had seen Mary.

A. You won't believe what a three-year-old girl asked me today!

B. What did she ask you?

A. She asked me why there was a Santa Claus in every department store in town.

B. I can't believe she asked you that!

A. I can't either.

A. You won't believe what a taxi driver asked me today!

B. What did he ask you?

A. He asked me $\left\{ \begin{array}{c} \text{if} \\ \text{whether} \end{array} \right\}$ I knew how to fix a flat tire.

B. I can't believe he asked you that!

A. I can't either.

A. You won't believe what _____ asked me today!

B. What did ____ ask you?

A. ____ asked me _____.

B. I can't believe _____ asked you that!

A. I can't either.

1. *my math teacher*

2. *my boyfriend*

3. *my employees*

4. *my students*

Have you ever been arrested?

5. *the woman at my job interview*

6. *my philosophy professor*

7. *my nine-year-old nephew*

8. *my basketball coach*

9. *our downstairs neighbors*

10. *my daughter*

11. *my parents*

12. *my boss*

13. *my son*

14. *one of my patients*

15. *a door-to-door salesman*

16.

He said,	He told me
"Call me after five o'clock."	. . . to call him after five o'clock.
"Stop smoking!"	. . . to stop smoking.
"Don't worry!"	. . . not to worry.
"Don't call me before nine o'clock."	. . . not to call him before nine o'clock.

A. I'm a little annoyed at the mailman.

B. How come?

A. He told me to keep my dog in the house.

B. Why did he tell you that?

A. He said (that) he was afraid to deliver my mail.

A. I'm a little annoyed at my English students.

B. How come?

A. They told me not to give them any homework this weekend.

B. Why did they tell you that?

A. They said (that) they were tired of English grammar.

A. I'm a little annoyed at _____.

B. How come?

A. ___ told me _____.

B. Why did _____ tell you that?

A. _____ said (that) _____.

1. *my doctor*

2. *my girlfriend*

3. *the school-bus driver*

4. *my dentist*

5. *my neighbors across the hall*

6. *my teacher*

7. *my nurse*

8. *my boss*

9. *my parents*

10. *my seven-year-old son*

11. *my landlord*

12. *my neighbors across the street*

ON YOUR OWN

1. Do you remember the last time somebody said something that really annoyed you?

What did the person say?
(He/She told me . . .)
Why do you think he/she said that?
Did you say anything back?

Talk about this with other students in your class.

2. "Bob would be angry if somebody told him he didn't play baseball very well."
"Patty would be upset if her parents told her to stop watching TV."
"Mike would be jealous if his girlfriend told him she wanted to go out with other boys."

Do YOU get angry, upset or jealous very easily? Complete these sentences and discuss with other students in your class:

1. I would be angry if _____ told me _____.
2. I would be upset if _____ told me _____.
3. I would be jealous if _____ told me _____.

Tag Questions
Emphatic Sentences

John **is** here, **isn't** he?	Yes, he **is**.	No, he **isn't**.
You **were** sick, **weren't** you?	Yes, I **was**.	No, I **wasn't**.
Maria **will** be here soon, **won't** she?	Yes, she **will**.	No, she **won't**.
Bobby **has** gone to bed, **hasn't** he?	Yes, he **has**.	No, he **hasn't**.
You like ice cream, **don't** you?	Yes, I **do**.	No, I **don't**.
Henry worked yesterday, **didn't** he?	Yes, he **did**.	No, he **didn't**.

Read and practice.

A. The bus stops at this corner, doesn't it?

B. Yes, it does.

A. That's what I thought.

1. You live in apartment seventeen, _____?

2. I can smoke here, _____?

3. Abraham Lincoln was our sixteenth president, _____?

4. You locked the front door, _____?

5. The President is going to speak on TV tonight, _____?

6. Miss Smith will be out of town next week, _____?

7. We've already seen this movie, _____?

8. You were a waiter in the restaurant across the street, _____?

9. You're a famous movie star, _____?

John **isn't** here, **is** he?	Yes, he **is**.	No, he **isn't**.
You **weren't** angry, **were** you?	Yes, I **was**.	No, I **wasn't**.
Sally **won't** be late, **will** she?	Yes, she **will**.	No, she **won't**.
You **haven't** eaten, **have** you?	Yes, I **have**.	No, I **haven't**.
George **doesn't** smoke, **does** he?	Yes, he **does**.	No, he **doesn't**.
They **didn't** leave, **did** they?	Yes, they **did**.	No, they **didn't**.

A. Your son isn't allergic to penicillin, is he?

B. No, he isn't.

A. That's what I thought.

1. The children don't ride this old bicycle any more, _____?

2. We didn't have any homework for today, _____?

3. I can't have any more candy, _____?

4. You aren't really going to go swimming today, _____?

5. The mail hasn't come yet, _____?

6. There weren't any airplanes when you were a little boy, _____?

7. Dr. Anderson won't be in the office tomorrow, _____?

8. I shouldn't take these pills right after I eat, _____?

9. I haven't taught "tag questions" before, _____?

A. You like to dance, don't you?

B. No, I don't.

A. You DON'T?! I'm really surprised!
I was SURE you liked to dance!

A. This park isn't dangerous at night, is it?

B. Yes, it is.

A. It IS?! I'm really surprised!
I was SURE this park wasn't dangerous at night!

1. A. It's going to be a nice day
tomorrow, _____?

B. No, _____.

2. A. The children aren't asleep yet,
_____?

B. Yes, _____.

3. A. This building has an elevator, _____?

   B. No, _____.

4. A. I don't have to wear a tie in this restaurant, _____?

   B. Yes, _____.

5. A. The post office hasn't closed yet, _____?

   B. Yes, _____.

6. A. You can swim, _____?

   B. No, _____.

7. A. I did well on the exam, _____?

   B. No, _____.

8. A. Dolphins can't talk, _____?

   B. Yes, _____.

9. A. The earth is flat, _____?

   B. No, _____.

10. A. I wasn't going over fifty-five miles per hour, _____?

   B. Yes, _____.

11. A. We have a spare tire, _____?

   B. No, _____.

12. A. You won't be offended if I don't finish your delicious cake, _____?

   B. Yes, _____.

CONGRATULATIONS!

A. I have some good news!

B. What is it?

A. My wife and I are celebrating our fiftieth wedding anniversary tomorrow!

B. You ARE?!

A. Yes, we are.

B. I don't believe it! You aren't REALLY celebrating your fiftieth wedding anniversary tomorrow, are you?

A. Yes, it's true. We ARE!

B. Well, congratulations! I'm very glad to hear that!

A. I have some good news!

B. What is it?

A. I got a fifty-dollar-a-week raise!

B. You DID?!

A. Yes, I did.

B. I don't believe it! You didn't REALLY get a fifty-dollar-a-week raise, did you?

A. Yes, it's true. I DID!

B. Well, congratulations! I'm very glad to hear that!

1. I won the lottery!

2. I'm going to have a baby!

3. I've been promoted!

4. The mayor wants me to paint his portrait!

5. I'm going to be the star of the school play!

6. We've found the man who robbed your house!

7. I can tie my shoes by myself!

8. My daughter has been accepted to Harvard University!

9. We won the football championship today!

10. I was interviewed by *The New York Times* yesterday!

11. I've discovered the cure for the common cold!

12.

Mary is late.
George was angry.
They aren't very friendly.
I don't know the answer.

They work hard.
John looks tired.
Janet came late to class.

Mary IS late.
George WAS angry.
They AREN'T very friendly.
I DON'T know the answer.

They DO work hard.
John DOES look tired.
Janet DID come late to class.

A. You know . . . the color blue looks very good on you.

B. Come to think of it, you're right!
The color blue DOES look very good on me, doesn't it.

A. You know . . . it isn't a very good day to fly a kite.

B. Come to think of it, you're right!
It ISN'T a very good day to fly a kite, is it.

1. . . . you work too hard.

2. . . . Rover is a very talented dog.

3. . . . Uncle Frank hasn't called in a long time.

4. . . . that was an awful movie.

5. . . . this milk tastes sour.

6. . . . you have quite a few gray hairs.

7. . . . we really shouldn't be hitchhiking at night.

8. . . . Lesson 19 is easier than Lesson 18.

9. . . . little Bobby talks in much longer sentences now.

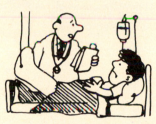

10. . . . you won't be able to play soccer for several months.

11. . . . you've been talking on the telephone for a long time.

12. . . . our English teacher gave us a lot of homework last night.

13. . . . our grandchildren don't write as often as they used to.

14. . . . the choir sang beautifully this morning.

15. . . . your brother Peter and my sister Margaret would probably make a nice couple.

16. . . . you did your homework very carelessly.

17. . . . this new toaster doesn't work very well.

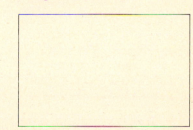

18.

Read and practice.

He's She's It's	late, isn't	he she. it	We're You're They're	late, aren't	we you. they	**I'm** late, **aren't** I.

*

A. You're in a bad mood, aren't you.

B. In a bad mood? What makes you think I'm in a bad mood?

A. Well, you shouted at me a few minutes ago.

B. Now that you mention it, I guess I DID shout at you a few minutes ago, didn't I.

A. You're_____, aren't you.

B. _____? What makes you think I'm_____?

A. Well,_____.

B. Now that you mention it, I guess_____, _____ _____.

Complete these conversations and try them with other students in your class.

1. *nervous*

2. *angry*

3. *upset*

4. *bored*

5. *embarrassed*

6. *jealous*

Review:
Verb Tenses
Conditionals
Gerunds

Read and practice.

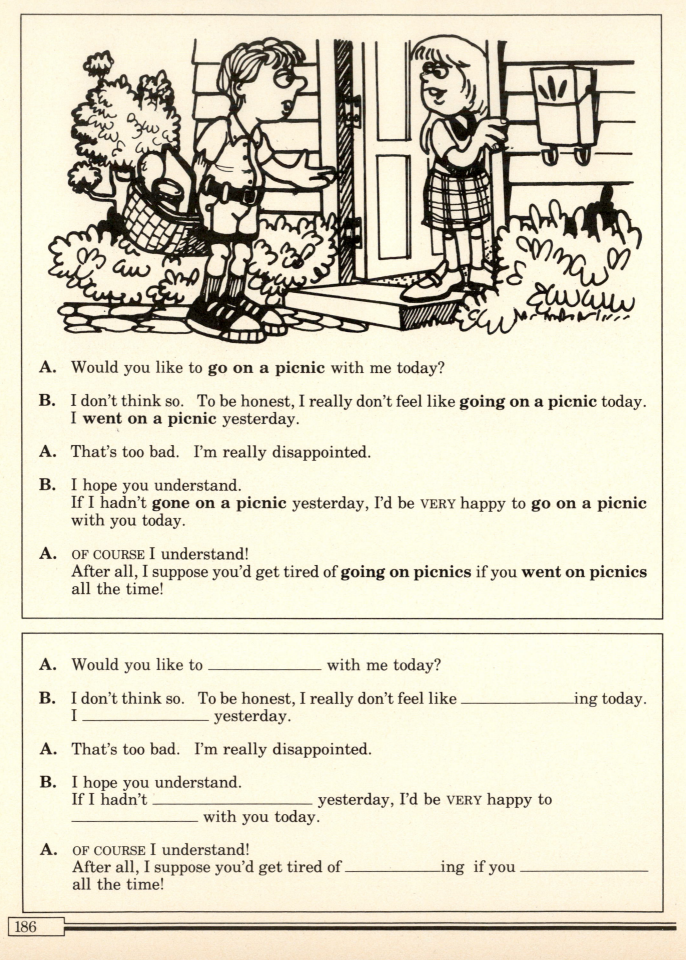

A. Would you like to **go on a picnic** with me today?

B. I don't think so. To be honest, I really don't feel like **going on a picnic** today.
I **went on a picnic** yesterday.

A. That's too bad. I'm really disappointed.

B. I hope you understand.
If I hadn't **gone on a picnic** yesterday, I'd be VERY happy to **go on a picnic**
with you today.

A. OF COURSE I understand!
After all, I suppose you'd get tired of **going on picnics** if you **went on picnics**
all the time!

A. Would you like to _____ with me today?

B. I don't think so. To be honest, I really don't feel like _____ing today.
I _____ yesterday.

A. That's too bad. I'm really disappointed.

B. I hope you understand.
If I hadn't _____ yesterday, I'd be VERY happy to
_____ with you today.

A. OF COURSE I understand!
After all, I suppose you'd get tired of _____ing if you _____
all the time!

1. *swim*

2. *see a movie*

3. *go dancing*

4. *play chess*

5. *eat at a restaurant*

6. *drive around town*

7. *study Algebra*

8. *go shopping*

9. *take a walk in the park*

10.

A. Do you realize what you just did?

B. No. What did I just do?

A. You just **ate both our salads**!

B. I did?

A. Yes. You did.

B. I'm really sorry. I must have **been very hungry**.
If I hadn't **been very hungry**, I NEVER would have **eaten both our salads**!

1. *drive past my house*
forget your address

2. *step on my feet*
lose my balance

3. *go through a red light*
be daydreaming

4. *hit me with your umbrella*
be looking the other way

5. *paint the living room window*
have my mind on something else

6. *call me Gloria*
be thinking about somebody else

7. *drink all the milk in the refrigerator*
be really thirsty

8. *throw out my homework*
think it was scrap paper

9. *put my pen in your pocket*
think it was mine

10. *put tomatoes in the onion soup*
misunderstand the recipe

11. *give Mr. Smith's medicine to Mr. Jones*
mix up Mr. Jones and Mr. Smith

12. *sit on my cat*
think it was a pillow

A. You seem upset. Is anything wrong?

B. Yes. **The heating system in my building is broken.**

A. I'm sorry to hear that.
How long **has it been broken?**

B. **It's been broken** for **two days**.

A. I know how upset you must be.
I remember when **the heating system in MY building was broken.**
Is there anything I can do to help?

B. Not really. But thanks for your concern.

A. You seem upset. Is anything wrong?

B. Yes. _____.

A. I'm sorry to hear that.
How long _____?

B. _____ (for/since) _____.

A. I know how upset you must be.
I remember when _____.
Is there anything I can do to help?

B. Not really. But thanks for your concern.

1. My best friend is angry at me.

2. My father is in the hospital.

3. My TV is broken.

4. My girlfriend wants to break up with me.

5. I'm unemployed.*

6. The elevator in my apartment building is out of order.

7. I'm having trouble sleeping at night.

8. My landlord refuses to fix my bathtub.

9. My dog is lost.

10. My wisdom teeth hurt.

11. I have cockroaches in my apartment.

12. I'm having trouble communicating with my teenage daughter.

*You can also say: I'm out of work.

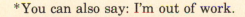

A. Hello, Bob. This is Sam.

B. Hi, Sam. How are you?

A. I'm O.K.
Listen, Bob . . . I'm trying to **put in my air-conditioner**, but I'm having trouble **putting it in** by myself. Could you possibly come over and give me a hand?

B. I'm really sorry, Sam. I'm afraid I can't come over right now.
My relatives are visiting from Chicago.
If **my relatives weren't visiting from Chicago**, I'd be GLAD to help you **put your air-conditioner in**.

A. Don't worry about it.
If I had known **your relatives were visiting from Chicago,**
I wouldn't have even called you in the first place!

A. Hello, _____. This is _____.

B. Hi, _____. How are you?

A. I'm O.K.
Listen, _____ . . . I'm trying to _____, but I'm having trouble _____ing by myself. Could you possibly come over and give me a hand?

B. I'm really sorry, _____. I'm afraid I can't come over right now.
_____.
If _____, I'd be GLAD to help you _____.

A. Don't worry about it.
If I had known _____,
I wouldn't have even called you in the first place!

1. hang up a portrait of
   my grandfather
   "I'm late for a job interview."

2. fix my stove
   "I have a bad cold."

3. move my piano
   "I have to wait for the plumber."

4. figure out our math homework
   *"I have to help my parents clean
   our apartment."*

5. repair my bedroom window
   *"My boss and her husband
   are coming for dinner."*

6. find one of my contact lenses
   "I'm on my way to church."

7. pick out new wallpaper
   for my kitchen
   *"I have to take care of my
   neighbor's daughter."*

8. fill out an application
   for a bank loan
   *"Both my children are
   home sick today."*

9. replace the cold water faucet
   in my bathroom sink
   *"I'm just about to take my wife
   to the hospital."*

10.

DECISIONS

Read and practice.

Several years ago, my friends urged me not to quit my job at the post office. They told me that if I quit my job there, I would never find a better one.

I didn't follow their advice . . . and I'm glad that I didn't. I decided to quit my job at the post office, and found work as a chef in a restaurant downtown. I saved all my money for several years, and then opened a small restaurant of my own. Now my restaurant is famous, and people from all over town come to eat here.

I'm glad I didn't listen to my friends' advice. If I had listened to their advice, I probably never would have opened this restaurant and become such a success.

My brother thought I was crazy when I bought this car. He told me that if I bought this car, I'd probably have lots of problems with it.

I didn't follow his advice . . . and I'm really sorry I didn't. Since I bought this car two months ago, I've had to take it to the garage for repairs seven times.

I wish I had listened to my brother. If I had listened to him, I never would have bought such a "lemon"!

My ski instructor insisted that I was ready to try skiing down the mountain. I told him that I was really scared and that I thought I needed much more practice. He told me I was worrying too much, and that skiing down the mountain wasn't really very dangerous.

I decided to take his advice. I began to ski down the mountain, but after a few seconds, I lost my balance and crashed into a tree.

I wish I hadn't listened to my ski instructor. If I hadn't listened to him, I wouldn't be lying here in the hospital with my leg in a cast.

Do you remember a time when you had to make an important decision and people gave you lots of advice?

Talk with other students in your class about the advice people gave you and the decision you made:

What did people tell you?
Why did they tell you that?
Did you follow their advice?
What happened?
Do you think you made the right decision? Why or why not?

APPENDIX

Irregular Verbs

Irregular Verbs

be	was	been
become	became	become
begin	began	begun
bite	bit	bitten
blow	blew	blown
break	broke	broken
bring	brought	brought
build	built	built
buy	bought	bought
catch	caught	caught
choose	chose	chosen
come	came	come
cost	cost	cost
cut	cut	cut
do	did	done
draw	drew	drawn
drink	drank	drunk
drive	drove	driven
eat	ate	eaten
fall	fell	fallen
feed	fed	fed
feel	felt	felt
fight	fought	fought
find	found	found
fit	fit	fit
fly	flew	flown
forget	forgot	forgotten
forgive	forgave	forgiven
freeze	froze	frozen
get	got	gotten
give	gave	given
go	went	gone
grow	grew	grown
hang	hung	hung

have	had	had
hear	heard	heard
hide	hid	hidden
hit	hit	hit
hold	held	held
hurt	hurt	hurt
keep	kept	kept
know	knew	known
lead	led	led
leave	left	left
lend	lent	lent
let	let	let
light	lit	lit
lose	lost	lost
make	made	made
mean	meant	meant
meet	met	met
put	put	put
quit	quit	quit
read	read	read
ride	rode	ridden
ring	rang	rung
run	ran	run
say	said	said
see	saw	seen
sell	sold	sold
send	sent	sent
set	set	set
sew	sewed	sewed/sewn
shake	shook	shaken
shrink	shrank	shrunk
sing	sang	sung
sit	sat	sat
sleep	slept	slept

speak	spoke	spoken
spend	spent	spent
stand	stood	stood
steal	stole	stolen
sweep	swept	swept
swim	swam	swum
take	took	taken
teach	taught	taught
tell	told	told
think	thought	thought
throw	threw	thrown
understand	understood	understood
wake	woke	woken
wear	wore	worn
win	won	won
wind	wound	wound
write	wrote	written

Index

A

B